Andy Saunderson is a cookery writer with a focus on recipes that help to alleviate skin conditions, such as psoriasis, psoriatic arthritis and eczema. *The Psoriasis Cook* is Andy's first book and he explores the impact that diet has on these medical conditions. His narrative includes a list of foods to avoid and foods that are recommended to soothe these conditions naturally, followed by over 100 modern and accessible recipes.

This book is dedicated to my mum for all of her help throughout the years, and to Kerry for her encouragement and support in getting this book to publication.

Andy Saunderson

The Psoriasis Cook

A Nine-Stage Healing Process

AUSTIN MACAULEY PUBLISHERS™
LONDON * CAMBRIDGE * NEW YORK * SHARJAH

Copyright © Andy Saunderson 2021

The right of Andy Saunderson to be identified as author of this work has been asserted by the author in accordance with section 77 and 78 of the Copyright, Designs and Patents Act 1988.

All rights reserved. No part of this publication may be reproduced, stored in a retrieval system, or transmitted in any form or by any means, electronic, mechanical, photocopying, recording, or otherwise, without the prior permission of the publishers.

Any person who commits any unauthorised act in relation to this publication may be liable to criminal prosecution and civil claims for damages.

A CIP catalogue record for this title is available from the British Library.

ISBN 9781528998857 (Paperback)
ISBN 9781528998864 (Hardback)
ISBN 9781528998871 (ePub e-book)

www.austinmacauley.com

First Published 2021
Austin Macauley Publishers Ltd
Level 37, Office 37.15, 1 Canada Square
Canary Wharf
London
E14 5AA

I would like to thank a number of people that have provided me with a lot of support during this project. Before I sat down to begin working on the book, I had a view that writing one must be quite a lonely exercise, but it hasn't felt that way at all, quite the opposite actually.

In no particular order, I would like to thank the following people that have been present in one way or another during the writing of this book. I would like to thank Mum, Dad, Paul and Mark for their constant interest in what I was doing and where I was up to with the project, providing support and encouragement along the way. I would like to thank Kerry for giving me the encouragement I needed to finally complete the project, collaborating with me on how to present the book and for doing such a great job at editing it for me. To my friends for providing a welcomed distraction when required – Oscar, Verdy, Samuel, Nicholas, Robert, Ben, David and Jeffs. Thank you also to Kelly, Rowena, Aneurin, Alys and Mari.

Finally, a mention to Dr John Pagano for writing the book that provided me with the inspiration to look at my diet differently, which has ultimately led to me writing this book.

Thank you all x

Introduction

I've had psoriasis for over 25 years, from just a few small patches in my early teens to being almost completely covered in my mid-20s.

My annual visits to the doctor had never brought up any surprises. No new advancements in medicine that eradicated my skin condition. I'd tried ointments, creams, steroids and phototherapy, but nothing ever worked.

In lieu of any changes, I decided to look at whether there were any alternative therapies out there. There were many companies ready to take my money in exchange for remedies that, in my experience, didn't provide me with anything that I hadn't been offered by my doctor or dermatologist.

During this period of investigation, I did read a number of things which provided me with some hope. There was a consensus that psoriasis could be managed in a different way and treated by healing from within.

Psoriasis has been described as being the result of an over abundant accumulation of toxins in the body which are released through the skin. The skin eliminates these toxins in the form of psoriasis. So, in order for me to treat my psoriasis, a different approach was to get to the root cause and heal the condition internally.

The internal cleansing was achieved by eliminating these toxins which had accumulated over a number of years. It involved exploring the foods I eat, concentrating on a high alkaline, low acid forming diet. It also included drinking various herbal teas and taking supplements to assist in healing my gut.

I set out by listing all of the foods to avoid completely, then all of the foods which were allowed, highlighting those which were highly recommended. I explored additional things to incorporate into my diet and daily routine, in particular, juices and herbal teas. I devised a variety of dishes that would be suitable throughout the year and substituted foods that weren't recommended, meaning that my compromise wasn't an extreme one.

From devising, cooking and eating my recipes, I have discovered that altering my diet has had an extremely positive impact on my psoriasis. Making these changes has enabled me to take greater control of my psoriasis and with this book, I hope it will enable you to do the same.

P.S.O.R.I.A.S.I.S
A Nine-Stage Healing Process

P.S.O.R.I.A.S.I.S = Problem, Solution, Organise, Reduce, Increase, Achieve, Start, Implement and Sustain.

These are the various stages that I went through during the process of healing my psoriasis from within.

This is a guide that you can use to take ownership of your psoriasis.

The 9 stages are:

Problem – Psoriasis and a build-up of toxins in the body.

Solution – A high alkaline and low acid diet.

Organise – Shopping, planning for meals and incorporating cooking into your life.

Reduce – Food and drink which are not good for you and your psoriasis.

Increase – Your intake of what is good for you.

Achieve – A reduction in irritation and inflamed skin.

Start – A new habit of not saying 'I'll start again on Monday'.

Implement – All of these changes into your life to take control of your psoriasis.

Sustain – Healthier looking skin and an improved quality of life.

Problem

Psoriasis is an autoimmune disease and skin condition which causes red, flaky patches of skin. The cause of psoriasis has never been confirmed, nor has a cure ever been found in traditional medicine. An alternative view is that psoriasis is triggered from an increased level of toxins in your body which seep through your intestinal wall. When the wall becomes thin, toxins can leak through into your bloodstream and circulate throughout your body, accumulating in your body's cells.

The process of toxins escaping through your porous intestinal wall is called **Leaky Gut Syndrome**. Accumulated toxins force your liver and kidneys to overwork in order to get rid of them. Sooner or later these organs are unable to flush the toxins out. Your skin comes to the rescue in eliminating the toxins from your body in the form of psoriasis patches.

Solution

The solution is to eat fresh whole foods – fruit, vegetables, meat, fish, pulses and grains.

All varieties of food and drink are either alkaline forming or acid forming. The aim is to consume a diet which consists of 70%–80% alkaline formers and 20%–30% acid formers. Filling your diet with alkaline formers will alter the pH levels within your body and your blood will be more on the alkaline side, which is much better for your health.

The following pages contain a list of alkaline and acid forming foods. Numerous lists like this exist, all with slightly different results, but on the whole, they share the following themes:

Most alkaline: Vegetables
Neutral: Fruit, nuts, grains & pulses
Most acidic: Red meat, processed foods and alcohol

Highly alkaline:
   Broccoli
   Cucumber
   Kale
   Parsley
   Spinach

Moderately alkaline:
   Almonds
   Avocado
   Basil
   Beetroot/beets

- Butter beans
- Cabbage
- Celery
- Chestnuts
- Chives
- Collard/spring greens
- Coriander
- Fennel
- Garlic
- Ginger
- Green beans
- Haricot beans
- Lettuce
- Lemon
- Lime
- Maple syrup
- Onions
- Parsnips
- Quinoa
- Rocket/arugula
- Spring onions/scallions
- Squash
- Sweet potatoes

Mildly alkaline:

- Almond milk
- Artichokes
- Asparagus
- Avocado oil
- Brussel sprouts
- Buckwheat
- Carrots
- Cauliflower
- Coconut
- Coconut oil
- Courgette/zucchini

Grapefruit
Herbs & spices
Leeks
Lentils
Olive oil
Peas
Rhubarb
Spelt
Swede/rutabaga
Tofu
Watercress

Neutral/mildly acidic:

Black beans
Brazil nuts
Brown rice
Cherries
Chick peas
Couscous
Fresh dates
Fresh water wild fish
Grapeseed oil
Hazelnuts
Honey
Kidney beans
Melon
Mushrooms
Nectarine
Oats
Pecan nuts
Plums
Soy milk
Soybeans
Sunflower oil
Pomegranate

Moderately acidic:

- Apple
- Apricots
- Banana
- Blackberries
- Blueberries
- Chicken
- Cranberries
- Gluten-free bread
- Grapes
- Honey
- Lamb
- Mango
- Orange
- Peach
- Pear
- Pistachio nuts
- Prunes
- Raisins
- Rye bread
- Tamari
- Tinned fruit
- Turkey
- Wheat
- Wine

Highly acidic:

- Beef
- Beers & spirits
- Canned meat & fish
- Coffee
- Dairy
- Dried fruit
- Jam / Jelly
- Mustard
- Peanuts

Pork
Processed foods
Shellfish
Sweets/candy
Tea
Vinegar
Walnuts
White flour products

Organise

It is helpful to have a plan of how you will incorporate a healthy diet into your life. By organising your grocery shopping and meals, you will save food waste as you'll be buying what you need and nothing more, which will save you money.

Batch cooking

Whenever I make dishes such as any type of ragu, sauce or soup, I purposely make too much so that I can freeze a few portions. Having these in the freezer for those times when you arrive home late and don't feel like cooking can be a lifesaver when you need something quick and nutritious.

Kitchen appliances

There are a couple of essentials which I use in my kitchen that I would definitely recommend. The first is a food processor. The one I own is at the budget end of the scale and offers a great alternative to finely chopping onions, carrots and celery and does so in a fraction of the time. The blender attachment is also perfect for blitzing soups to a smooth consistency.

The other essential is a juicer. Owning a juicer and getting into the habit of making your own vegetable juice is a means of adding the nutrients from alkaline vegetables into your body on a daily basis.

Reduce

The following are a list of foods and drinks that are considered to have an adverse effect on psoriasis.

Nightshades:

- Aubergine/eggplant
- Chillies
- Goji berries
- Peppers/paprika/cayenne pepper
- Tobacco
- Tomatoes
- White potatoes

The above are to be avoided completely. There are conflicting reports as to why nightshades are harmful for people with psoriasis. Some believe that it is due to the way your body processes the vitamin D found in nightshades, other reports suggest that it's down to how your gut reacts to the alkaloids found within them.

Red meat

Highly acidic, high in saturated fat and the protein in red meat is harder for you to break down. Improper digestion of meat can lead to an accumulation of toxins in the body.

Whilst it is advisable to cut red meat out completely, I do still eat it on occasion. I limit my intake to only having it once a week at most. Lamb is the least acidic red meat, so I usually opt for that.

Full fat dairy

Dairy has been known to cause inflammation; therefore, I have reduced my intake considerably by opting for a mix of lower fat versions and plant-based products. If dairy is a trigger for you, try eliminating it completely – there are many dairy-free alternatives listed in the recipes in this book.

Gluten

The question of whether gluten has an adverse impact on psoriasis is a contentious one as it seems to for some people and not others. Based on this, I have decided to be more mindful of my intake of gluten and opt for gluten-free options wherever possible.

Aside from whether reducing my intake of gluten has had an impact on my skin, I definitely feel less bloated as a result of reducing my intake of it. There are now a wide range of gluten-free alternatives to bread, flour and pasta so I would recommend making that change in your diet.

If gluten isn't an issue for you, try replacing all white flour products with whole grain alternatives.

Shellfish

Shellfish contains high levels of purine. When your body digests purine, it produces a waste product called uric acid. In psoriasis, uric acid is considered to be a by-product of rapid skin cell turnover and systemic inflammation.

Caffeine

Caffeine dehydrates your body, but not to the same extent as alcohol. I reduced my intake to 1 cup of coffee per day and replaced it with herbal teas at other times of the day.

Alcohol

A number of skin problems have been linked to excessive alcohol consumption, mainly due to the damage caused to various organs.

Psoriasis plaques are patches of dry, flaky skin. Alcohol's effect is that it will dry your skin even further. Alcohol consumption leads to dehydration, vitamin deficiency and can impact your immune system.

I cannot stress enough how important it is to reduce your alcohol intake if you are to be successful in clearing your skin. I have cut down my intake of alcohol considerably to an occasional glass of red wine on the weekend. The reason I did this was because I didn't want to give up alcohol completely, and because beer, spirits and white wine always seemed to have an adverse effect on my skin.

Junk food

Junk food contains a lot of saturated fat, sugar, preservatives and has a much lower nutritional value than fresh food. It lacks the necessary nutrients you require to remain energized and healthy.

Junk food impairs your digestion, largely due to the high levels of acidity, which can damage your vital organs. This should be completely avoided.

Processed meat

This refers to meat which has been preserved by curing, salting, smoking, drying or canning. It includes bacon, ham, sausages, hot dogs, salami, salted and cured meat, corned beef, smoked meat and dried meat.

Processed meat is generally considered unhealthy, it contains many harmful chemicals which are not present in fresh meat and excessive amounts of salt, preservatives and fat.

Strawberries

Strawberries can cause an adverse reaction for some people; therefore, I try to avoid them.

Food combinations to avoid

- Citrus with dairy
- Raw apples, bananas or melons with other foods
- Wholegrain products with citrus
- Fruit with white flour products
- Try to avoid adding milk to tea or coffee
- Do not combine too many acid-forming foods during a meal

Psoriatic arthritis and eczema

There are a few different considerations for cases of psoriatic arthritis and eczema:

· Dairy is to be completely avoided in cases of eczema
· Avoid salt in cases of psoriatic arthritis
· Avoid citrus fruits and juices in cases of psoriatic arthritis and eczema – therefore, adapt any recipes in this book to omit citrus – apple cider vinegar is a good alternative.

Increase

The following are a list of foods and drinks that are considered to have a positive effect on psoriasis.

Herbal teas

A cup of herbal tea is one of the best things you can drink. There are a wide variety of them on the market which contain various blends of herbs, fruits, flowers and roots. These teas also consist of a range of vitamins, minerals and antioxidants which are beneficial to your health and in particular to help clear your skin. They help with boosting your immune system, improving your digestion and reducing inflammation.

Recommended teas
Chamomile tea

Chamomile tea is full of antioxidants and is particularly good for flushing out the system as well as helping with sleep.

American saffron

This tea detoxifies the digestive tract, helping to heal the intestinal walls.

Water

It is such an essential part of your basic functioning. Water raises your energy levels by stimulating your muscles, boosts productivity by sustaining your brain and supports your immunity and metabolism. It assists in the removal of toxins and waste from your body, which helps with digestion and clearing your skin.

Granular lecithin

Lecithin is recommended to be taken 3 times a day, 5 days a week. Granular form is recommended and it can be added to any liquid, food or taken by itself. It is beneficial for digestion and your skin in general.

Juicing

Why should you be buying a juicer and not a blender?

The main difference is that juicing separates the juice from the fibre, whereas with blending, you get everything. Juicing is better for this diet because it removes the pulp and whilst you may be removing a lot of fibre, what you're left with is the nutrient rich juice which goes directly into the bloodstream without the need for digestion.

I didn't include fruits in the juices as I wanted to avoid the high fructose fruits and keep calories to a minimum. Drinking juices are not a meal replacement. It is a daily routine to boost your intake of vegetables. Taking in all of those nutrients will help lower cholesterol, lower blood sugar levels and improve your energy levels.

Omega 3 supplements

These are recommended due to them being effective in the regeneration and reconstruction of the intestinal wall. Omega 3 supplements also help with hydrating your skin and reducing inflammation.

Alkaline foods

I am aware that I've included information about alkaline foods earlier on within the solution section, but I will reiterate the point that it is important to increase your intake of alkaline foods.

Achieve

Once you are on your way with cooking more, eating foods which are better for you, including alkaline vegetables on a daily basis, you will hopefully start to see some positive results.

How soon and pronounced will differ from each individual to the next. It will depend greatly on a number of factors, including how drastic the change is from what your eating and drinking habits have previously been, it will also depend on how rigid you are with implementing the recommendations that I have listed.

The differences that I noticed a few weeks into doing this were – I felt healthier in general, had more energy, my skin was less irritable, and over time, the psoriasis showed signs of dissipating. For me, it worked on a system of last in, first out. The newest psoriasis patches I had cleared first – within a few weeks. The oldest psoriasis patches that I'd had for a number of years took a few months to improve.

This is not a quick fix whereby you do something for a few weeks and then go back to old habits. It can take a while for you to see any benefits from this. But if you continue, it will have a positive effect on you, your skin and your overall well-being.

Start

I'll start again on Monday. You've said it and I've said it.
Whether it's trying to stop smoking, maintaining a diet or exercising more, we have all been sent off course and thought or said 'I'll start again on Monday'.

There will always be challenges that make this new way of eating difficult to stick to. These challenges could be eating out with friends or celebrating milestones. Accepting that, from time to time other events will prevent you from being able to maintain the new regime rigidly should help with keeping in the right mindset.

The best approach I have found is to be flexible as opposed to being rigid. If you are able to maintain this regime 95% of the time and avoid saying 'I'll start again on Monday', then you will be applying the changes to your daily life.

Implement

Below is a summary of how you can incorporate the recommendations into your daily life.

Daily plan

Granular lecithin

Lecithin is recommended to be taken 3 times a day, 5 days a week. Add it to any liquid, food or take it by itself.

Omega 3

Take these supplements with your breakfast to help with restoring and repairing the intestinal wall.

Vegetable juice

Try to have a vegetable juice once a day to increase your intake of vegetables and to absorb them directly into your bloodstream.

Herbal teas

Try to have a cup of chamomile or American Saffron tea each evening to flush out the system.

Snacking

Whilst you are considering implementing a new daily routine into your life, it feels only right to include a few words on snacking.

When you are trying to avoid all processed foods, refined sugar, and generally anything which is bad for you, snacking can feel quite limiting. Fresh fruit is always a good option to replace crisps/chips or chocolate, as are nuts and seeds as well.

Sustain

Hopefully the biggest motivator will be feeling better and noticing improvements in your skin. This is a nine-stage plan which shows what you can do to take ownership of improving your skin and health in general.

The feeling of taking responsibility for your skin and health can be very empowering. Especially when there did not seem to be any answers on how to clear psoriasis.

By looking at your diet and altering it, you can take full ownership of your psoriasis. You can also sustain a healthier diet and lifestyle by cutting out foods that are bad for you.

Breakfast & Brunch

Gluten-Free Porridge with a Blueberry Compote & Mixed Seeds

The working days of the week are when time is scarce, but breakfast is essential, therefore I need something quick, filling and nutritious. Porridge oats tend to be the go-to option during this period of the week as it ticks all of those boxes.

Serves 2

Ingredients:

Gluten-free porridge oats/oatmeal: 90g/1 cup
Almond milk: 500ml/2 cups

For the blueberry compote:
Frozen blueberries: 100g/3 ½ oz
Water: 2 tablespoons
Granulated sugar: A pinch

To serve:
Chai seeds: 2 teaspoons
Pumpkin seeds: 2 teaspoons
A drizzle of honey or maple syrup

Method:

1. For the compote, add the blueberries to a saucepan on the hob over a low heat. Add a couple of tablespoons of water to the pan and a pinch of

sugar. Heat gently for 10 minutes until the blueberries have broken down.
2. Add the oats and milk to a separate saucepan on the hob over a low to medium heat. Cook for 5 minutes or so, until the porridge is thickened and the oats have softened. Top with the compote, seeds and honey.

Overnight Oats

Perfect for those days in the week when you don't have much time to spare for breakfast. You can make these oats the night before, it only takes a few minutes to put together and it means that breakfast for the following morning is taken care of. It's also easily transportable so you can take it with you if you don't have time to eat at home.

Serves 1

Ingredients:

    Gluten-free porridge oats/oatmeal: 45g/½ a cup
    Low fat milk or dairy-free alternative: 125ml/½ a cup
    Low fat yoghurt or dairy-free alternative: 125ml/½ a cup
    Chai seeds: 1 teaspoon
    Mixed berries: 125g/1 cup

Method:

1. Add the oats to a container and mix in the milk and yoghurt. Top with the fruit and scatter the seeds. Cover and refrigerate overnight.
2. Serve the following morning.

Beetroot Hummus with Avocado & Hazelnut Dukkah

Beetroot is packed full of antioxidants and works really well here with the usual hummus ingredients. The quantities in this recipe makes enough hummus to have leftovers. The dukkah is optional and can be made in advance – the recipe quantity is much more than you'll need for this recipe but it will keep in an airtight container for a few weeks and offers a great fragrance and texture to liven up the dish.

Serves 4

Ingredients:

For the hummus:
- Chickpeas: 1 x 400g/15 oz can
- Cooked beetroot: 250g/9 oz, chopped
- Tahini: 2 tablespoons
- Garlic: 1 clove, minced
- Extra virgin olive oil: 2 tablespoons
- Pink Himalayan salt: ½ teaspoon
- Lemon: Juice of ½

For the dukkah:
- Blanched hazelnuts: 100g/3½ oz
- Cumin seeds: 2 tablespoons
- Coriander seeds: 2 tablespoons
- Fennel seeds: 2 tablespoons
- Sesame seeds: 4 tablespoons
- Pink Himalayan salt: 2 teaspoons

For the rest:

Avocados: 2, scooped from their skin, stoned/pitted, halved and sliced
Gluten-free bread: 4 thick slices, toasted

Method:

1. Preheat the oven to 180°C/fan 160°C/350°F/gas mark 4.
2. For the dukkah, mix all of the ingredients together in a bowl and then spread evenly on a baking tray. Cook in the oven for 10 minutes until toasted.
3. Tip the toasted dukkah into a food processor and pulse a few times to break the nuts up a little. Transfer to an airtight container, it'll keep for a few weeks.
4. Add all of the hummus ingredients to a food processor and process until smooth. You may need to use a spatula to incorporate any of the mix that sticks to the side when processing. Give it a good mix and process again until smooth. Add a few tablespoons of chilled water to the mix until you reach a consistency that you are happy with.
5. Spread the hummus over the toast, top with avocado, a scattering of the dukkah and serve.

Green Smoothie Bowl

Smoothie bowls are a relatively new concept. They are a great way of packing fruit and vegetables into a meal and they are very quick to put together. This means that they are a great option for a midweek breakfast, when you might be a bit more pushed for time.

Serves 1

Ingredients:

For the smoothie:
- Almond milk: 180ml/ ¾ cup
- Avocado: ½, chopped
- Kiwi fruit: 2, peeled and sliced
- Ginger: 1 slice, peeled
- Spinach: 2 large handfuls

Toppings:
Fresh blueberries, chai and pumpkin seeds

Method:

1. Add all of the smoothie ingredients to a blender and blend until smooth.
2. Add to a bowl and serve, topped with the berries and seeds.

Chive Polenta with Sautéed Chestnut Mushrooms & Kale

Polenta is a great ally to have when thinking about different dishes to make for the psoriasis diet. I've used it tirelessly during the time I've been devising recipes. Here I've gone for something to bulk out a brunch recipe with mushrooms. The recipe can be easily halved, and if you don't have time to make the polenta, you can use gluten-free bread instead.

Serves 4

Ingredients:

For the polenta:
   Polenta: 200g/7 oz
   Vegetable stock: 800ml/3¼ cups
   Chives: 4 tablespoons
   Olive oil: 1 tablespoon

For the mushrooms:
   Portobello or chestnut mushrooms: 400g/14 oz, wiped clean and sliced
   Butter or dairy-free alternative: 1 tablespoon
   Olive oil: 1 tablespoon
   Garlic: 1 clove, minced
   Kale: 200g/7 oz, chopped
   Chives: 2 tablespoons

To serve:
   Eggs: 4, poached

Method:

1. Line a 20cm x 30cm baking tray with cling wrap.
2. Add the vegetable stock to a pan and gradually whisk in the polenta, stirring until well mixed.
3. Cook for 2–3 minutes then stir in the chives and season well with salt & pepper. Tip the polenta onto the tray, spread out and smooth the surface. Leave to cool, then cover and chill for at least 30 minutes, although it can be left overnight.
4. Preheat a griddle pan on the hob over a medium heat.
5. Turn the chilled polenta out onto a chopping board and cut into 8 wedges. Lightly oil each wedge and cook on the griddle pan for 4–5 minutes on each side until cooked and nicely charred.
6. For the mushrooms, get a frying pan/skillet on the hob over a medium heat and add the butter and oil. Add the mushrooms, garlic, kale and begin to fry, giving them a shake every minute or so. As they fry, they'll release water and intensify in flavour. After about 5 minutes, they should be almost ready, add the chives and season with salt & pepper.
7. Serve with a couple of wedges of the griddled polenta and a poached egg.

Gluten-Free American Style Blueberry Pancakes with Maple Syrup

An American breakfast staple, these work just as well with gluten-free flour. Thick, spongy and great served with a drizzle of maple syrup.

Serves 4

Ingredients:

    Gluten-free self-raising flour: 200g/7 oz
    Baking powder: 2 teaspoons
    Caster/superfine sugar: 1 tablespoon
    Eggs: 2, beaten
    Milk or dairy-free alternative: 300ml
    Fresh blueberries: 150g/5 oz
    Olive oil: 2 tablespoons
    Maple syrup: A good drizzle

Method:

1. Add the flour, baking powder, sugar and a pinch of salt to a mixing bowl.
2. Add the eggs and milk into the mixing bowl and whisk well until you have a smooth batter, then fold in half of the blueberries.
3. Heat a large frying pan/skillet over a medium heat and add a touch of olive oil to it.
4. Put a heaped tablespoon of the mixture into the pan, repeat 2–3 times until you fill the pan and cook for 2–3 minutes on each side or until

golden. Keep warm in a low oven while you repeat the process for the remaining mixture.
5. Serve the pancakes with a scattering of blueberries and a drizzle of maple syrup.

Corn & Courgette Fritters with Avocado, Pesto, Toasted Seeds & Poached Egg

The title of this may be a bit of a mouthful but it's straightforward enough to put together. The main thing to keep an eye on is the batter mix for the fritters; you don't want it to be too wet so make sure you completely drain the corn and courgette and you should be fine. It's a colourful plate too, vibrant and full of a range of textures to kick-start your day.

Serves 2

Ingredients:

- Buckwheat or other gluten-free flour: 50g/2 oz
- Olive oil: 1 tablespoon
- Baking powder: ½ teaspoon
- Eggs: 1, beaten
- Milk or dairy-free alternative: 60ml/¼ cup
- Spring onions/scallions: 2, thinly sliced
- Sweetcorn/corn: 198g/7 oz can (drained weight approx. 165g/6 oz)
- Courgette/Zucchini: 1, grated
- Fresh mint: 1 tablespoon, chopped

To serve:

- Almond pesto: 2 tablespoons
- Avocado: 1, peeled, stoned/pitted and sliced
- Pumpkin or mixed seeds: A scattering
- Eggs: 2, poached

Method:

1. Sift the flour and baking powder into a bowl.
2. Add the eggs, milk and whisk well until you have a smooth batter.
3. Mix in the spring onions/scallions, corn, courgette, mint and give everything a good mix. Season with salt & pepper.
4. Heat a large frying pan/skillet over a medium heat and add a tablespoon of olive oil to it.
5. Put a heaped tablespoon of the mixture into the pan, repeat until you have 4 fritters and cook for 2–3 minutes on each side or until golden.
6. Serve the fritters in the middle of the plate with some chopped avocado, a drizzle of pesto, a scattering of pumpkin seeds and top with a poached egg.

Root Vegetable Hash with a Poached Egg

This is a brunch that reminds me of Christmas. It is a family tradition to have any leftover vegetables from Christmas Day for breakfast on Boxing Day. I love it, so much so that instead of just having it whenever there are any leftover vegetables, I'll go out of my way to make the 'leftover' veg as an excuse to make this for brunch.

Serves 2

Ingredients:

>Olive oil: 1 tablespoon
>Onion: 1, chopped
>Fresh spinach: 100g/3½ oz
>Leftover root veg mash (carrot, swede/rutabaga, sweet potato or parsnip): 400g/14 oz
>Butter or dairy-free alternative: 1 tablespoon
>Eggs: 2, poached

Method:

1. Heat the oil in a frying pan/skillet on the hob over a low heat, add the onion and cook for 10 minutes. Add the spinach and cook for a further 5 minutes. Remove and add to a mixing bowl with the leftover root veg.
2. Season with salt & pepper and then shape into four patties.
3. Heat the butter and a touch more oil in a frying pan/skillet over a medium heat and fry the patties for 5 minutes on each side until golden and crisp.
4. Serve topped with a poached egg.

Green Veg Brunch Frittata – Broccoli, Kale, Pea & Chive

This is called a brunch frittata but the good thing is that you could have it at any time of the day. Full of green veg to fill your body with those all-important alkaline foods.

Serves 3–4

Ingredients:

    Olive oil: 2 tablespoons
    Tender stem broccoli: 200g/7 oz, chopped
    Kale: 100g/3½ oz, chopped
    Frozen peas: 100g/3½ oz
    Fresh chives: 4 tablespoons, chopped
    Eggs: 6, beaten

Method:

1. Preheat the oven to 200°C/fan 180°C/400°F/gas mark 6.
2. Warm the olive oil in an oven safe frying pan/skillet on the hob over a medium heat.
3. Add the chopped broccoli and sauté for 5 minutes until it begins to soften. Add the kale, frozen peas and sauté for another 5 minutes. Add the eggs, chives and season with salt & pepper. Mix well and bake in the oven for 15 minutes until it's set and golden brown.
4. Cut into wedges and serve.

Indian-Style Scrambled Eggs

I first came across this way of making scrambled eggs in a cookbook given to me as a gift one Christmas. Admitttedly, the recipe was packed with chilli and fresh tomatoes, which I've obviously omitted for my version.

Serves 2

Ingredients:

>**Eggs: 6, beaten**
>**Butter or dairy-free alternative: 1 tablespoon**
>**Olive oil: 1 tablespoon**
>**Cumin seeds: ½ teaspoon**
>**Yellow mustard seeds: ½ teaspoon**
>**Onion: 1 small, diced**
>**Fresh ginger: Thumb sized piece, grated**
>**Ground turmeric: ½ teaspoon**
>**Fresh chives: 2 tablespoons**
>**Gluten-free bread: 2 slices, toasted**

Method:

1. Get a frying pan/skillet on the hob over a medium heat and add the butter and oil. Add the cumin, mustard seeds, onion, ginger and fry for a few minutes.
2. Add the turmeric to the pan along with some salt & pepper and give everything a good mix before adding in the beaten eggs.
3. Continue to mix until the eggs are cooked to your liking. When they are, serve with some toast and a scattering of fresh chives.

Juices

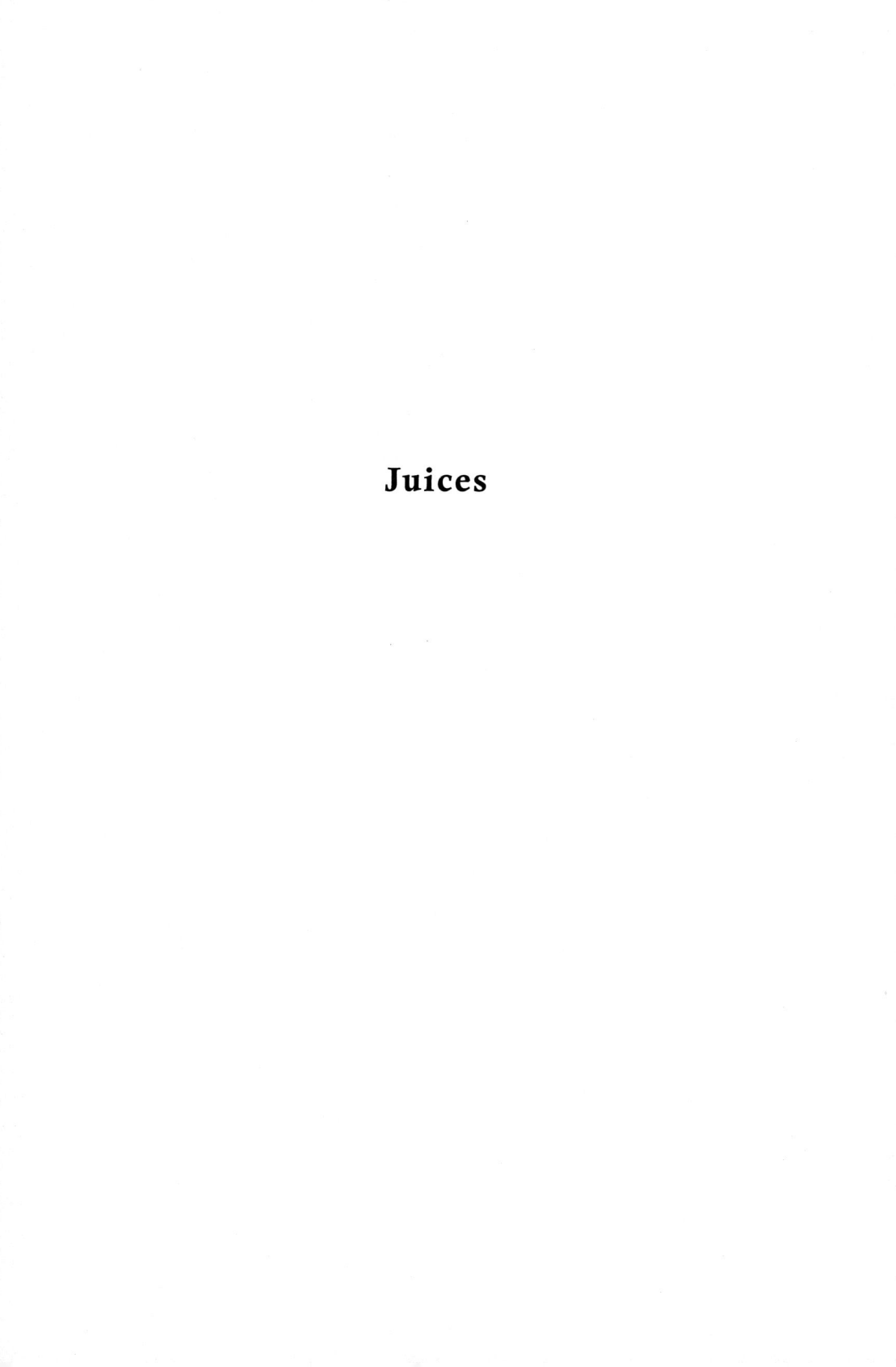

There are many good reasons for juicing your own vegetables – the obvious one is that you know you are getting pure vegetable juice directly into your bloodstream.

The cost savings are staggering compared to how much vegetable juices cost in the supermarket. You can make your own juice for a fraction of the cost of a shop bought one. It will also be fresher, you will have a bigger choice of vegetables to use and only takes a couple of minutes to make.

One thing I do want to address is the difference between juicing and blending, just in case it is a cause of confusion for you. The main difference between the two is that juicing separates the juice from the fibre, whereas with blending, you get everything. Of the two options, juicing is better for this diet because the juice is transferred directly into your bloodstream without going through the breakdown process.

All of the juice recipes that follow are merely ideas; feel free to add whatever vegetables you have to hand. When making a juice, I always try to include green leafy vegetables as they are highly recommended for clearing your skin.

Try to incorporate one glass a day into your life. I usually make my juices the night before and leave them in the fridge for the next morning. It's easier and helps me stay on track with ensuring I have one each day.

Cucumber, Kale, Spinach & Ginger Juice

Serves 1

Ingredients:

Cucumber: ¼, chopped
Kale: 1 handful
Spinach: 1 handful
Ginger: A thumb-sized piece

Method:

1. Pass all of the ingredients through a juicer and then top up with some mineral water and serve.

Carrot, Ginger & Romaine Lettuce Juice

Serves 1

Ingredients:

Carrots: 3, chopped
Ginger: A thumb-sized piece
Romaine lettuce: 1/2, chopped

Method:

1. Pass all of the ingredients through a juicer and then top up with some mineral water and serve.

Beetroot, Carrot, Celery & Ginger Juice

Serves 1

Ingredients:

Raw beetroot: 1, peeled and chopped
Carrots: 2, chopped
Celery: 2 sticks, chopped
Ginger: A thumb-sized piece

Method:

1. Pass all of the ingredients through a juicer and then top up with some mineral water and serve.

Romaine, Carrot, Celery & Beetroot Juice

Serves 1

Ingredients:

Romaine lettuce: 1/2, chopped
Carrots: 2, chopped
Celery: 2 sticks, chopped
Raw beetroot: 1, peeled and chopped

Method:

1. Pass all of the ingredients through a juicer and then top up with some mineral water and serve.

Broccoli, Cucumber, Celery & Spinach Juice

Serves 1

Ingredients:

Broccoli: 1 handful
Cucumber: ¼, chopped
Celery: 2 sticks, chopped
Spinach: 1 handful

Method:

1. Pass all of the ingredients through a juicer and then top up with some mineral water and serve.

Cucumber, Carrot, Celery & Kale Juice

Serves 1

Ingredients:

Cucumber: ¼, chopped
Carrot: 2, chopped
Celery: 2 sticks, chopped
Kale: 1 handful

Method:

1. Pass all of the ingredients through a juicer and then top up with some mineral water and serve.

Soups & Smaller Plates

Celery, Onion & Spinach Soup

The virtues of a nourishing bowl of soup contributed to the birth of the restaurant. During the 18th century, a new kind of establishment opened in Paris, with tables and menus. It specialised in bowls of soups, said to be restoratives – food that restores.

Soups are easy to make and can be packed full of alkaline forming vegetables that are so beneficial to us. This soup dishes up plenty of those leafy greens that are so vital to our diet. While this soup is achingly healthy, it's also quite tasty. A good option for this and other soups is to batch cook them and freeze any leftovers for another time.

Serves 3–4

Ingredients:

> **Olive oil: 2 tablespoons**
> **Onions: 2, chopped**
> **Celery: 6 stalks, chopped**
> **Fresh spinach: 240g/9 oz**
> **Garlic: 2 cloves, minced**
> **Vegetable stock: 1 litre/4 cups**

Method:

1. Heat the oil in a large pot on the hob over a low heat.
2. Add the onions and celery, season with salt & pepper and sweat for 10 minutes. Add the garlic and sweat down for a further 5 minutes.

3. Add the stock, turn up the heat and bring to the boil, then reduce the heat and simmer for 10 minutes.
4. Add the spinach, allow to wilt down for a few minutes until well mixed, then transfer to a blender and blend until smooth before serving with a scattering of seeds.

Italian Inspired Courgette & Rocket Soup

There are some classic combinations on show here. Even though they usually go together in a salad, they also work in a soup. If putting rocket/arugula in a soup is something new to you, it works well, giving the soup a slightly peppery taste.

Serves 2

Ingredients:

- Olive oil: 1 tablespoon
- Garlic: 1 clove, minced
- Courgettes/zucchini: 500g/18 oz, sliced
- Vegetable stock: 500ml/ 2 cups
- Fresh basil leaves: 1 handful
- Fresh rocket/arugula: 1 handful

To garnish (optional):
- A drizzle of extra virgin olive oil

Method:

1. Heat the oil in a large pot on the hob over a low heat.
2. Add the courgette/zucchini and soften for 5 minutes. Season with salt.
3. Add the garlic, basil, rocket/arugula and cook for another 5 minutes until the courgettes/zucchini are softened.
4. Add the stock and simmer for 10 minutes.

5. Pour the soup into a blender and blend until smooth. For added texture on the finished soup, remove a few pieces of courgette/zucchini prior to blending. If the soup is too thick for you, add a little water.
6. Return to the pan and stir in the reserved courgettes/zucchini and check the seasoning, adding more salt & pepper to taste.
7. To serve, ladle the soup into bowls.

Sweet Potato & Red Lentil Soup

Sweet potato and red lentils give this soup it's velvety thickness. The immune boosting ginger gives it a welcomed kick, finished off perfectly with the freshness of coriander/cilantro and lime.

Serves 3–4

Ingredients:

    Olive oil: 2 tablespoons
    Onions: 2, sliced
    Garlic: 2 cloves, minced
    Fresh coriander/cilantro: 1 handful, stalks reserved
    Fresh ginger: Thumb sized piece, grated
    Sweet potato: 600g/21 oz, peeled and chopped
    Veg stock: 1 litre/4 cups
    Red lentils: 100g/3½ oz
    Lime: Juice of 1

Method:

1. Heat the oil in a large pot on the hob over a low heat and add the onions. Cook for 10 minutes then add the ginger, garlic and cook for another 5 minutes.
2. Add the coriander/cilantro stalks, lentils, sweet potato, stock and cook for 20 minutes or until the lentils and sweet potato is cooked.
3. Blend until smooth, adding a little more stock or water if the consistency is too thick for you. Check the seasoning, adding salt & pepper as required, then add the coriander/cilantro, lime juice and serve.

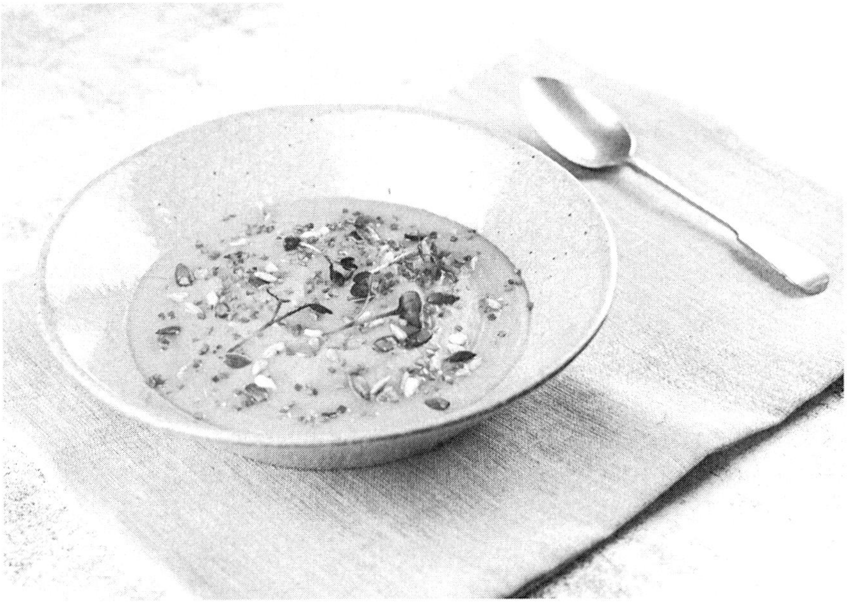

White Minestrone

Not much has changed from the classic minestrone, I've just omitted the tomatoes and changed the white pasta for gluten-free pasta. If the only minestrone you've ever previously had is from a can, you really should give this a go as it's packed full of flavour.

Serves 4

Ingredients:

    Olive oil: 2 tablespoons
    Carrots: 1, peeled and finely diced
    Celery: 2 sticks, finely diced
    Onion: 1, finely diced
    Garlic: 2 cloves, minced
    Fresh rosemary: 2 sprigs, finely chopped
    Fresh thyme: 2 sprigs, finely chopped
    Kale: 50g/2 oz, finely chopped
    Chicken or vegetable stock: 1.5 litres/6 cups
    Borlotti beans: 1 x 400g/15 oz can
    Gluten-free spaghetti: 50g/2 oz, cut into small pieces
    Pesto: 4 tablespoons, for drizzling (optional)

Method:

1. Heat the oil in a large pot on the hob over a low heat and add the carrot, onions and celery and sweat down for 15 minutes.
2. Add the garlic, kale, rosemary, thyme and cook for another 5 minutes.

3. Add the stock, spaghetti and beans. Bring to the boil and simmer for 30 minutes.
4. Check the seasoning, adding salt & pepper as required then serve in bowls with a drizzle of pesto.

Mushroom & Kale Soup

A perfect lunch for those autumn or winter months. This earthy, wholesome mushroom soup is given an extra hit of goodness from the addition of kale.

Serves 3–4

Ingredients:

- **Olive oil: 2 tablespoons**
- **Onions: 1, chopped**
- **Celery: 2 sticks, chopped**
- **Kale: 100g/3½ oz**
- **Garlic: 2 cloves, minced**
- **Rosemary: 2 sprigs, leaves picked**
- **Mixed mushrooms: 500g/18 oz, sliced**
- **Chicken or vegetable stock: 1.5 litres/6 cups**

Method:

1. Heat the oil in a large pot over a gentle heat and sweat the onions and celery for 10 minutes. Season with salt & pepper then add the garlic, kale, mushrooms, rosemary and fry for another 5 minutes.
2. Add the stock and mix well. Simmer for 15–20 minutes.
3. Blend everything together then add some more salt & pepper if necessary. Serve with a light scattering of mixed seeds.

Cauliflower & Kale Soup with Crispy Kale

Back to another green(ish) soup. Yet again, it's filled with those all-important green vegetables. Here, we've got the addition of cauliflower to give it a luxurious texture when blended, the sort of texture that you only usually get from adding cream to a soup.

Serves 3–4

Ingredients:

Olive oil: 2 tablespoons
Onions: 1, sliced
Celery: 2 stalks, chopped
Garlic: 2 cloves, minced
Cauliflower: 1, outer leaves removed and cut into florets
Kale: 100g/3½ oz
Veg stock: 1 litre/4 cups
Pine nuts: 2 tablespoons, toasted
For the crispy kale (optional)
Kale: 50g/2 oz
Olive oil: 1 tablespoon

Method:

1. Heat the oil in a large pot on the hob over a low to medium heat and add the onions, celery and cook for 15 minutes.
2. Add the garlic, kale, cauliflower and cook for a further 5 minutes.

3. Add the stock, bring to the boil and simmer for 20 minutes or until the cauliflower is cooked.
4. Blend until smooth and return to the pan, adding a little more stock if the consistency is too thick for you. Check that you're happy with the seasoning and serve with a scattering of toasted pine nuts and crispy kale.
5. Whilst you're making the soup, if you want to make the crispy kale, preheat the oven to 170°C/fan 150°C/325°F/gas mark 3.
6. Mix the kale with the oil, season with salt & pepper and place on a baking tray. Bake for 20 minutes until crispy. Use as a topping for the soup.

Harira – Chickpea & Lentil Stew

A popular soup in Morocco, this recipe is a bit more like a stew in its consistency and makes for quite a substantial meal, especially when served with some gluten-free flatbreads.

Serves 2–3

Ingredients:

- Onion: 1, finely chopped
- Celery: 2 sticks, finely chopped
- Olive oil: 1 tablespoon
- Fresh ginger: Thumb sized piece, peeled and grated
- Ground turmeric: 2 teaspoons
- Ground cinnamon: 1 teaspoon
- Nutmeg: ½, grated
- Chickpeas: 1 x 400g/15 oz can
- Dried green lentils: 100g/3½ oz
- Vegetable stock: 750ml/3 cups
- Courgette/zucchini: 1, quartered and sliced
- Lemon: Juice of ½
- A mixed handful of fresh parsley and coriander/cilantro

Method:

1. Heat the olive oil in a large pot on the hob over a low heat, add the onion, celery and cook for 10 minutes. When the onions and celery have softened, add the ginger and cook for another 5 minutes.

2. Add the turmeric, cinnamon, nutmeg and stir for 1 minute, then add the green lentils, chickpeas and veg stock. Turn up the heat and bring to boil, then reduce and simmer for 30 minutes, or until the lentils are just about cooked but still have a slight bite to them. During the cooking time, keep an eye on the pan to make sure that the stock doesn't evaporate. If required, add some water to top it up.
3. When the lentils are just about cooked, add the fresh herbs, courgette/zucchini and salt & pepper to taste. Cook for 5 minutes and serve on its own or with some flatbreads.

Roast Chicken, Quinoa & Asparagus Salad with a Chive & Basil Dressing

This is a great salad to make use of asparagus when it is in season. Chicken and asparagus are a classic combination, add a creamy dressing to the mix and you have all of the component parts for a great lunch.

Serves 2

Ingredients:

For the salad:
Quinoa: 50g/2 oz
Olive oil: 1 tablespoon
Chicken breasts: 2, skinless
Cucumber: Half, sliced into half moons
Asparagus: 150g, chopped
Spinach: Two handfuls

For the dressing:
Dairy-free yoghurt: 100g/3½ oz, sliced
Fresh chives: A small bunch, about 13g, sliced
Fresh basil: A small bunch, about 13g, sliced
Lemon juice: 1 tablespoon
Honey: 1 teaspoon

Method:

1. Boil the quinoa according to the packet instructions. Two minutes before the cooking time is up, add the asparagus to the pot. Drain and leave to one side.
2. Preheat the oven to 200°C/fan 180°C/400°F/gas mark 6.
3. Heat the oil in an oven safe frying pan/skillet on the hob over a medium heat.
4. Season the chicken with salt & pepper and add to the pan and brown for 3 minutes each side.
5. Transfer the pan to oven and cook for 15–20 minutes or until the chicken is cooked. Allow to cool and then slice.
6. Add all of the dressing ingredients to a blender or food processor and blend until smooth. Season with salt & pepper.
7. Add the cucumber to a mixing bowl, along with the spinach, cooked quinoa, asparagus, chicken and dressing.
8. Give everything a good mix and divide between two bowls and serve.

Brown Lentil, Truffle Oil & Chestnut Mushroom Pate

This is a great alternative to a usual pate as they're usually very rich with butter and meat. The earthy mushrooms, walnuts and lentils deliver a great taste and texture for this dish. Truffle oil isn't for everyone so if you're not keen, simply omit it from the recipe.

Serves 6

Ingredients:

>Chestnut mushrooms: 100g/3½ oz, sliced
>Olive oil: 2 tablespoons
>Onion: 1, peeled and chopped
>Garlic: 2 cloves, minced
>Brown lentils: 175g/6 oz
>Walnuts: 150g/5 oz
>Fresh lemon: Juice of ½
>Truffle oil: 1 tablespoon
>Fresh rosemary: 2 tablespoons
>Fresh parsley: 2 tablespoons

Method:

1. Cook the lentils as directed on the packet instructions. When cooked, drain and allow to cool.
2. While that is underway, heat the olive oil over a medium heat in a frying pan/skillet. Add the onions and cook for 10 minutes. Add the garlic and

cook for another 5 minutes. Add the rosemary, mushrooms and cook for another 10 minutes until the mushrooms are cooked.
3. Remove the pan from the heat and allow the mixture to cool slightly, before adding to a food processor along with the lentils and other ingredients. Blitz until the mixture is smooth, check the seasoning, adding additional salt & pepper if required.
4. Transfer to a terrine dish lined with cling wrap and refrigerate for a few hours until firm.
5. Serve with gluten-free crackers or toast.

Carrot & Coriander Rosti with a Fresh Cucumber Salad

These rosti are great for a light, healthy lunch served with a fresh cucumber salad. Crispy rosti with a sweetness and earthiness to them that works perfectly with the refreshing cucumber. The flour helps to hold the mixture together when forming the rosti. You may need a little more or less than as stated in the recipe, depending on how wet the mixture is.

Serves 2

Ingredients:

For the rosti:
- Carrots: 300g/10½ oz, grated
- Spring onions/scallions: 4, sliced
- Fresh coriander/cilantro: 2 tablespoons approx.
- Eggs: 2, beaten
- Buckwheat or other gluten-free flour: 2 tablespoons
- Olive oil: 1 tablespoon

For the salad:
- Cucumber: ½, sliced lengthways
- Rocket/arugula: 2 handfuls
- Olive oil: 2 tablespoons
- Lemon: Juice of ½
- Mint leaves: A few, finely chopped

Method:

1. Grate the carrots and add to a mixing bowl with the spring onions/scallions and coriander/cilantro.
2. Add the beaten egg, flour and bind everything together. Season well with salt & pepper.
3. Take a heaped tablespoon of the mixture and shape into a rosti. Repeat for the rest of the mixture. You should get 4 rosti out of the mixture.
4. Heat a large frying pan/skillet and add the oil. When the oil is hot, add the rosti. Fry for 3–4 minutes on each side until golden brown. Try not to move them around too much in the pan, let the rosti form a crust before you turn them over.
5. For the salad, simply mix the olive oil and lemon together, then mix in the mint, rocket/arugula and cucumber. Serve the salad with the rosti.

Avocado & Broccoli Noodle Salad with an Asian Pesto

Changing the usual ingredients of a classic Italian pesto for a couple of different herbs and some Asian staples provides a great sauce to use as a base for this salad. It also works in stir fry's too so the quantity of the pesto could easily be doubled and stored in the fridge for 2–3 days.

Serves 2

Ingredients:

For the pesto:
- Fresh mint: 2 sprigs, leaves picked
- Fresh coriander/cilantro: A small bunch, leaves picked and chopped
- Fresh ginger: Thumb sized piece, peeled & chopped
- Fresh garlic: ½ a clove, minced
- Fresh lime: Juice of ½
- Tamari: 1 tablespoon
- Sesame oil: 1 tablespoon
- Spring onions/scallions: 1, sliced

For the salad:
- Rice or other gluten-free noodles: 100g/3½ oz
- Tenderstem broccoli: 200g/7 oz
- Avocado: 1, chopped
- Pumpkin or mixed seeds: A scattering

Method:

1. For the pesto, place all ingredients into a food processor and blitz until well combined.
2. Cook the noodles according to packet instructions and once done, drain and rinse in cold water to stop them from cooking.
3. Steam or boil the broccoli for 2–3 minutes and when cooked, mix with the avocado, pesto and noodles.
4. Scatter with some seeds and serve.

Chicken & Corn Quesadilla

This is a firm favourite of mine. As someone that loves Mexican food, this is clearly a nod in that direction. Even without the addition of chilli it still has all the characteristics of a quesadilla.

Serves 2

Ingredients:

Gluten-free tortillas: 4
- **Cooked chicken: 150g/5 oz, sliced**
- **Ground cumin: ½ teaspoon**
- **Spring onions/scallions: 6, chopped**
- **Fresh coriander/cilantro: 2 tablespoons, chopped**
- **Sweetcorn/corn: 198g/7 oz can (drained weight is approx. 165g/6 oz)**
- **Dairy-free yoghurt or crème fraiche: 2 tablespoons**

Method:

1. Put two tortillas onto a chopping board and spread half of the crème fraiche on them. Add the chicken, cumin, spring onions/scallions, coriander/cilantro and corn between the two and season with salt & pepper.
2. Put the remaining two tortillas onto a chopping board and spread the other half of the crème fraiche out on both of them, then place them on top of the side that has the filling.
3. Heat a frying pan/skillet over a moderate heat and add the first one to the pan carefully. Cook for about 5 mins until the tortilla has browned, pressing down gently so that it sticks together. Carefully turn it over and

cook on the other side for another 5 minutes. Remove and cut into quarters.
4. Repeat the process for the remaining one and serve them with some dressed leaves.

Fish

Sweet Potato & Smoked Mackerel Fishcakes with a Beetroot Salad

This is a fairly straightforward recipe to put together when you've already got the cold sweet potato left in the fridge. I usually plan my meals so that I can make a double quantity of sweet potato mash for some of the other recipes and then make these the following day. You can also freeze these fishcakes prior to cooking, making them a great meal to have on hand in the freezer.

Serves 3–4

Ingredients:

For the fishcakes:
- Cold mashed sweet potato: 300g/10½ oz
- Smoked mackerel: 250g/9 oz, skinned and flaked
- Spring onions/scallions: 6, sliced
- Dijon mustard: 1 teaspoon
- Buckwheat or other gluten-free flour: 2 tablespoons
- Eggs: 1, beaten
- Gluten-free breadcrumbs: 100g/3½ oz

For the salad:
- Cooked beetroot: 250g/9 oz, cut into wedges
- Spinach: 100g/3½ oz
- Celery: 2 sticks, sliced
- Walnut pieces: 50g/2 oz
- Lemon: Juice of ½
- Extra virgin olive oil: 4 tablespoons

Method:

1. In a mixing bowl, combine the potato, mackerel, mustard and onion. Season with salt & pepper and shape into 8 even sized fishcakes.
2. Get three bowls in a line, one with the flour, one with the egg and one with the breadcrumbs.
3. One by one, cover the fishcakes in the flour, then the egg, finally giving them a good coating of breadcrumbs. Once done, you can chill until ready to cook. Or at this stage, you could freeze them.
4. To cook them, heat a frying pan/skillet over a medium heat and add 1 tablespoon of olive oil. Gently fry for 5 minutes on each side until golden brown and cooked through.
5. For the salad, add the beetroot, spinach, celery and walnuts to a mixing bowl.
6. Make the dressing by mixing the lemon juice and oil together in a cup, season with salt & pepper and mix into the salad. Serve the salad with a couple of fishcakes per person.

Grilled Mackerel with Wholegrain Mustard & a Fennel Salad

Versatile and packed full of omega 3, the mackerel stands up well to the strong mustard in this recipe. The addition of fennel adds a wonderful freshness to the dish.

Serves 2

Ingredients:

For the mackerel:
   Mackerel fillets: 2, pin bones removed and skin scored
   Wholegrain mustard: 1 tablespoon

For the fennel salad:
   Fennel bulb: 1, finely sliced
   Rocket/arugula: A large handful
   Cucumber: ½, sliced lengthways

For the dressing:
   Extra virgin olive oil: 2 tablespoons
   Apple cider vinegar: 1 tablespoon
   Dijon mustard: 1 teaspoon

Method:

1. Brush the mackerel with the mustard and season with salt & pepper. Place under a preheated grill/broiler and cook for 2–3 minutes, then turn and cook for a further minute or until cooked through.

2. For the salad, mix all the salad ingredients in a large bowl. Mix the dressing ingredients together, season with salt & pepper, then add to the salad and mix well.
3. Serve the salad topped with the mackerel.

Seabass with Broccoli, Lentils & a Lemon Caper Dressing

All of the component parts for this recipe go really well together. I am a big fan of the precooked pouches of lentils that are readily available these days. They save time and effort for this recipe, which is easy to throw together.

Serves 2

Ingredients:

    Seabass fillets: 2, trimmed and skin scored
    Tender stem broccoli: 200g/7 oz
    Ready to eat puy lentils: 1 x 250g/9 oz pouch
    Capers: 2 tablespoons
    Lemon juice: 1 tablespoon plus a couple of gratings of the zest
    Olive oil: 2 tablespoons

Method:

1. Cook the broccoli in a pan of boiling water for 2–3 minutes. When the time is up, drain the broccoli and add to a mixing bowl. Season with salt, pepper and a touch of olive oil.
2. Season the fish with salt & pepper, place a frying pan/skillet on the hob over a medium heat and add a little olive oil to it. Add the fish, skin side down and press down on the fish to avoid them curling up.
3. Cook for 3–4 minutes, then turn over and cook for another minute until cooked. Place onto a plate.
4. Cook the puy lentils according to the packet instructions; this only usually takes a couple of minutes as you're only warming them through.

5. For the sauce, place the frying pan/skillet back on the hob and add the remaining olive oil. Add the capers and cook until they begin to crisp up. When that happens, add the lemon zest and juice. Finally, add the lentils and broccoli to the capers and give everything a good mix. Divide the lentil mixture between two plates, topping with the seabass and an extra squeeze of lemon juice to finish off.

Fish & Chips

A true British classic! Whilst there are differing tales of when fish and chips was first served up, the one thing that all of the stories have in common is that it was somewhere in England. This version removes the white potatoes, batter and deep-frying so it is a much healthier alternative.

Serves 4

Ingredients:

    For the chips:
    Polenta: 200g/7 oz
    Vegetable stock: 800ml/3¼ cups
    Olive oil: 2 tablespoons

For the fish:
    White fish fillets (haddock, cod or pollock work well: 4, skinless and boneless (approx. 150g/5oz each)
    Buckwheat or other gluten-free flour: 4 tablespoons
    Eggs: 2 beaten
    Gluten-free breadcrumbs: 100g/3½ oz
    Chopped parsley: 2 tablespoons

For the mushy peas:
    Frozen peas: 450g/1 lb
    Fresh mint: A few sprigs, leaves picked.
    Natural yoghurt or dairy-free alternative: 1 tablespoon

Method:

1. For the polenta chips, line a baking tray with cling wrap. Add the veg stock to a saucepan and gradually whisk in the polenta, stirring continuously until well mixed. Cook for 2–3 minutes and then season well. Tip the polenta into the tray, spread out and smooth the surface. Leave to cool, then cover and chill for at least 30 minutes, although it can be left overnight.
2. Preheat the oven to 220°C/fan 200°C/425°F/gas mark 7. Pour the oil into a baking tray and heat in the oven.
3. Turn the chilled polenta out onto a chopping board and cut into fat chips.
4. Add the chips to the baking tray and cook for 30 minutes, turning occasionally until crisp and golden.
5. For the fish, tip the flour into a bowl and season with salt & pepper.
6. Beat the eggs into a separate bowl. Add the breadcrumbs into yet another bowl along with the parsley.
7. One at a time, dredge the fish fillets in the flour, shake off any excess, then dip into the egg, and finally dredge in the breadcrumbs until completely coated. Repeat the process for the remaining fillets.
8. Heat half of the butter and oil in a frying pan/skillet over a medium to high heat. Add two pieces of fish and cook for 2–3 minutes, then flip and cook for another 3 minutes on the other side until golden. Repeat for the remaining fillets.
9. For the peas, boil them in salted boiling water for 3–4 minutes then drain and transfer to a blender with the mint and yoghurt. Blitz to a puree, check if it requires any salt & pepper and serve with the fish and some polenta chips.

Hake with Creamy White Beans

A simple dish to put together, which is a nod in the direction of Spanish cuisine as they often have similar dishes of white fish and beans.

Serves 2

Ingredients:

    Leeks: 4, finely sliced
    Fresh thyme: A few sprigs, leaves picked
    Garlic: 2 cloves, minced
    Olive oil: 2 tablespoons
    Vegetable stock: 250ml/1 cup
    Butter beans: 1 x 400g/15 oz can
    Fresh parsley: A small bunch, chopped
    Natural or dairy-free yoghurt: 1 tablespoon
    Hake fillets: 2, boneless
    Olive oil: 1 tablespoon

Method:

1. For the beans, heat the oil in a saucepan on the hob over a low heat and add the leeks, thyme and garlic. Fry gently for 10 minutes, until completely soft.
2. Turn up the heat and add the stock and beans. Bring to the boil then reduce the heat to a simmer for 5–10 minutes.
3. Add the parsley and yoghurt, mix well and season with salt & pepper.

4. For the hake, season the fillets with salt & pepper. Heat a frying pan/skillet over a medium heat and add the remaining 1 tablespoon of olive oil.
5. Add the hake fillets, skin side down to the pan and cook for 3–5 minutes until the skin crisps up. Turn and cook for another 3–5 minutes.
6. Add the beans to two bowls and top with the hake. Serve with a drizzle of extra virgin olive oil.

Tuna Nicoise

In place of tomatoes and new potatoes that are ever present in a nicoise, I've added more alkaline forming greens to this version of it.

Serves 2

Ingredients:

Eggs: 2, boiled
French/string beans: 100g/3½ oz, trimmed
Cucumber: ½, cut into half moons
Spring onions/scallions: 4, finely chopped
Black olives: 100g/3½ oz, pitted
Capers: 1 tablespoon
Baby gem lettuces: 2
Basil leaves: A few, roughly torn
Fresh tuna steak: 325g/12 oz

For the dressing:
Lemon juice: 1 tablespoon
Olive oil: 2 tablespoons
Apple cider vinegar: 1 teaspoon

Method:

1. Put the eggs in a pan of cold water and bring slowly to the boil. Simmer for 10 minutes, then plunge into a bowl of iced water.
2. Cook the beans in salted boiling water for 4–5 minutes until slightly tender. Drain, tip into iced water, then drain again and set aside.

3. For the tuna, place a frying pan/skillet on the hob over a medium heat and add 1 tablespoon of oil. Season the tuna generously with salt & pepper, then sear for 4 minutes, leaving it undisturbed in the pan to brown. Turnover and continue to cook for 4 minutes on the other side. This will give you very rare tuna. For medium, cook for 2 minutes more on each side and for well done, add another 4 minutes on each side. Set the tuna aside to rest for a few minutes.
4. To make the dressing, mix the vinegar, oil and lemon. Season with salt & pepper and then mix with all of the other ingredients and serve.

Salmon & Green Vegetable Tray Bake

Anything that's made in one pot, or in this case one tray is always going to be a good idea. This dish works as both a lunch dish or can easily be filled out for dinner by having some brown rice or cous on the side.

Serves 2

Ingredients:

- **Salmon: 2 x 200g/7 oz fillets**
- **Tender stem broccoli: 250g/9 oz**
- **Asparagus: 1 bunch, sliced**
- **French/string beans: 250g/9 oz**
- **Spring onions/scallions: 1 bunch, sliced**
- **Lemon: 1, sliced**
- **Olive oil: 2 tablespoons**

To serve:
Chive and basil dressing from the basics section

Method:

1. Preheat the oven to 200°C/fan 180°C/400°F/gas mark 6.
2. Add all of the ingredients to a baking tray that's big enough to house everything in a single layer. Give it all a good mix to ensure the oil has reached all of the ingredients. Season with salt & pepper and bake for 20 minutes.

3. After the 20 minutes, the salmon should be cooked and the vegetables nice and crispy. Divide the veg amongst two plates and place the salmon on top.
4. Serve with some grains of your choice and the chive and basil dressing from the basics section of the book.

Meat

Katsu Chicken Curry

One of the most popular dishes in Japan, the katsu curry differs from a typical curry in that the chicken is breaded and cooked separately to the sauce. Obviously, chilli has been omitted so it's a mild curry, but katsu isn't known for being very spicy, so it doesn't feel like a compromise.

Serves 4

Ingredients:

    For the chicken:
    Buckwheat or other gluten-free flour: 4 tablespoons
    Eggs: 2, beaten
    Gluten-free breadcrumbs: 100g/3½ oz
    Chicken breasts: 4, skinless and boneless
    Olive oil: 2 tablespoons
    Butter or dairy-free alternative: 2 tablespoons
    For the sauce:
    Olive oil: 1 tablespoon
    Onion: 1, diced
    Fresh garlic: 2 cloves, minced
    Carrots: 1, diced
    Buckwheat or other gluten-free flour: 1 tablespoon
    Curry powder (see basics section): 1 tablespoon
    Chicken stock: 600ml/2½ cups
    Honey: 1 tablespoon
    Tamari: 1 tablespoon
    Garam masala (see basics section): 1 teaspoon

Method:

1. For the sauce, heat the oil in a saucepan over a low to medium heat and add the onion and carrot. Fry gently for 10 minutes, then add the garlic and fry for another 5 minutes.
2. Add the flour, curry powder and mix well, then gradually add in the chicken stock, mixing well to avoid any lumps.
3. Add in the honey and tamari, bring to the boil, then reduce the heat and simmer for 30 minutes.
4. After the 30 minutes add the garam masala and check the seasoning, adding salt & pepper as required.
5. At this stage the sauce is ready, and you can serve it as it is, or, if you prefer a smooth sauce, pass it through a sieve.
6. For the chicken, while the sauce is simmering away, preheat the oven to 200°C/fan 180°C/400°F/gas mark 6.
7. Season the chicken with salt & pepper.
8. Tip the flour into one bowl, beat the eggs into a separate bowl. Add the breadcrumbs into yet another bowl and you are ready to start.
9. One at a time, dredge the chicken in the flour, shaking off any excess, then dip into the egg, and finally dredge in the breadcrumbs until completely coated.
10. Heat half of the butter and oil in a frying pan/skillet over a medium to high heat. Add two pieces of chicken and cook for 2–3 minutes on each side until golden. Remove and place on a baking tray. Repeat for the remaining two pieces of chicken and once browned on each side, place in a preheated oven for 5–8 minutes until cooked through.
11. Serve the curry with brown rice and a dressed salad.

Roast Chicken with Chimichurri

Chimichurri is a piquant sauce that originated in Argentina. It usually contains chilli, but the dominant flavours are parsley and garlic.

Serves 4

Ingredients:

For the chicken:
Chicken breasts: 4, skinless
Olive oil: 2 tablespoons

For the chimichurri:
Flat leaf parsley: 30g, leaves picked and finely chopped
Apple cider vinegar: 2 tablespoons
Extra virgin olive oil: 6 tablespoons
Garlic: 1-2 cloves, minced
Dried oregano: 1 teaspoon

Method:

1. Preheat the oven to 200°C/fan 180°C/400°F/gas mark 6.
2. Heat the oil in an oven safe frying pan/skillet on the hob over a medium heat.
3. Season the chicken with salt & pepper and add to the pan and brown for 3 minutes each side.
4. Transfer the pan to the oven and cook for 15–20 minutes or until the chicken is cooked.

5. When it's cooked, remove the chicken from the oven and transfer it to a chopping board, cover in foil and rest for 5 minutes.
6. Add all of the chimichurri ingredients to a mini food processor and blitz until it's all combined, adding a little more oil if it's too thick. Check the seasoning, adding salt & pepper as required. Store in the fridge until you are ready to use it.
7. When the chicken is rested, cover with the chimichurri. Serve with a green salad and some polenta fries.

Za'atar Chicken Salad with Brown Rice

Za'atar is a readily available Middle Eastern herb mix that usually contains sesame seeds and a blend of oregano, thyme, marjoram and sumac. It's a great mix to have to hand for livening up your dishes. I've used it here as the marinade for a chicken dish, but it also works well scattered over a salad or hummus. Use whichever cut of the chicken you prefer.

Serves 2

Ingredients:

For the chicken:
Olive oil: 1 tablespoon
Chicken breasts: 2, skinless
Lime: Juice of ½
Za'atar: 2 tablespoons

For the salad:
Brown rice (uncooked): 100g/3½ oz
Frozen peas: 100g/3½ oz
Rocket/arugula: 100g
Fresh parsley: 2 tablespoons
Fresh mint: 2 tablespoons
Extra virgin olive oil: 1 tablespoon
Lemon: Juice of half
Sumac: 1 tablespoon

Method:

1. Mix the olive oil, lime juice and za'atar together and season with salt & pepper. Add the chicken and mix well. Cover and transfer to the fridge for at least 30 minutes.
2. Preheat the oven to 200°C/fan 180°C/400°F/gas mark 6.
3. Add the chicken to a baking dish and cook in the oven for 35–40 minutes, or until the chicken is cooked.
4. Whilst the chicken is underway, boil the brown rice according to packet instructions. 5 minutes before the end of the cooking time, add the peas to the pan. After the 5 minutes are up, drain and leave to one side.
5. Transfer the rice and peas to a mixing bowl and add in the rocket and herbs. Mix the oil and lemon juice together and add that to the mixing bowl too. Check if it needs any seasoning, adding some salt & pepper if required.
6. Divide the rice mixture between two plates and top with the chicken. Scatter a little sumac over both plates and serve.

Comforting Chicken & Mustard Casserole

A comforting casserole for those colder evenings, packed full of vegetables and held together by a thick mustard sauce. This casserole works well with some celeriac or sweet potato mash and a side of greens such as wilted spinach or sautéed kale.

Serves 3–4

Ingredients:

    Olive oil: 2 tablespoons
    Chicken thighs: 1 kg/2¼ lb, skinless, bone-in
    Onion: 1, finely diced
    Celery: 1 stick, finely diced
    Garlic: 2 cloves, minced
    Thyme: 3 sprigs, leaves only
    Carrots: 3, cut into 2cm pieces
    Buckwheat or other gluten-free flour: 1 tablespoon
    Wholegrain mustard: 1 tablespoon
    Chicken stock: 500ml/2 cups
    Flat leaf parsley: 2 tablespoons, chopped

Method:

1. Preheat the oven to 200°C/fan 180°C/400°F/gas mark 6.
2. Place a large oven safe pot on the hob over a medium heat and add half of the oil. Season the chicken with salt & pepper then add to the pot and brown until golden.

3. Remove the chicken and put to one side.
4. Lower the heat and add the remaining oil, onion, celery and thyme, cook for 10 minutes. After 10 minutes, add the garlic, carrots and cook for another 5 minutes.
5. Add the flour and give it a good mix, then add the mustard, stock and chicken thighs. Mix well then place a lid on and put in the oven for 30 minutes.
6. After 30 minutes, check that the chicken is cooked. If it isn't, give it another 5–10 minutes.
7. To serve, top the casserole with chopped parsley, check the seasoning, adding salt & pepper to taste. Serve with either some celeriac mash or brown rice and greens.

Chicken & Green Olive Tagine

This isn't quite a tagine, but it's pretty close. The two stars of the show are the olives and preserved lemons. Olives are a great ingredient; they've got a really sharp and salty flavour to them and the preserved lemons have a perfumed scent that really works well in this recipe.

Serves 3–4

Ingredients:

    Olive oil: 1 tablespoon
    Onion: 1, diced
    Garlic: 2 cloves, minced
    Fresh ginger: Thumb sized piece, minced
    Ground coriander: 1 teaspoon
    Chicken (skinless breasts or boneless thighs): 450g/1 lb
    Pitted green olives: 150g/5 oz
    Preserved lemons: 4, chopped
    Chicken stock: 500 ml/2 cups
    Flat leaf parsley: 2 tablespoons
    Spinach: 100g/3½ oz

Method:

1. Warm the oil in a large pot on the hob over a medium heat and add the onion. Season with salt & pepper and sweat down for 10 minutes, then add the garlic, ginger, coriander and sweat down for another 5 minutes. Add the chicken and seal the meat for 5–10 minutes.

2. Add the chicken stock, olives and lemons and turn up the heat to bring to the boil. Reduce the heat and cook for 20–30 minutes until all of the flavours have combined.
3. Add in the spinach and wilt for a couple of minutes. Finally add a scattering of the parsley and serve, either with some couscous or sweet potato mash.

Chicken & Black Pepper Curry

Devising a curry without chilli doesn't need to be a challenge. Black pepper is a great spice alternative and isn't a nightshade. Added to a familiar list of spices and you have a robust spice mix to use as the base for this fragrant curry, which works very well with the coconut milk.

Serves 3–4

Ingredients:

For the spice mix:
- Black peppercorns: 2 tablespoons
- Cumin seeds: 1 tablespoon
- Coriander seeds: 1 tablespoon
- Fennel seeds: 1 teaspoon
- Cloves: 5
- Olive oil: 2 tablespoons
- Ground turmeric: 2 teaspoons
- Lemon: Juice of ½

For the rest:
- Olive oil: 2 tablespoons
- Diced chicken thighs: 450g/1 lb
- Onions: 1, sliced
- Garlic: 2 cloves, minced
- Ginger: A thumb sized piece, grated
- Coconut milk: 400ml/1 ½ cup can
- Green beans: 200g/7 oz

Spinach: 250g/9 oz
Fresh coriander/cilantro: A handful

Method:

1. Heat a dry frying pan over a high heat and add the black peppercorns, cumin seeds, coriander seeds, fennel seeds, and cloves. Toast for 2–3 minutes without burning until fragrant, then remove and place in a pestle & mortar and grind until it's a fine powder.
2. Add the spices to a bowl along with the olive oil, turmeric and lemon juice. Mix well to combine everything and then add the chicken to marinade for a minimum of 30 minutes.
3. Heat the remaining oil in a deep casserole dish on the hob over a medium heat. Add the onions and cook for 10 minutes then add the garlic, ginger and cook for a further 5 minutes. Season with salt.
4. Add the marinated chicken and cook for 10 minutes, then mix in the coconut milk, green beans and simmer for 15 minutes.
5. Add the spinach and cook for a few minutes so that it wilts down.
6. When cooked, check the seasoning, adding more salt if required. Serve with a scattering of fresh coriander/cilantro and some brown rice.

Green Vegetables, Chicken & Brown Rice with a Spring Onion & Tahini Sauce

A healthy rice-based stir fry, full of alkaline forming green vegetables held together by a sesame-based sauce. The savoury tahini is balanced well with the salty tamari, citrus from the lime and finished with a fresh fragrance from the coriander/cilantro. This also works well with turkey. For the rice, either use precooked brown rice pouches or boil some ahead of cooking.

Serves 2

Ingredients:

For the sauce:
- Spring onions/scallions: 4, trimmed and sliced
- Fresh lime: Juice of ½
- Tamari: 1 tablespoon
- Sesame oil: 1 tablespoon
- Tahini: 1 tablespoon
- Fresh coriander/cilantro: 1 tablespoon

For the rest:
- Olive oil: 1 tablespoon
- Cooked brown basmati rice: 250g/9 oz
- Green vegetables: 3 handfuls (I used peas, spinach and kale)
- Skinless chicken thighs/breasts: 200g/7 oz, sliced
- Fresh coriander/cilantro: Handful, finely chopped
- White & black sesame seeds: 1 teaspoon of each to garnish

Method:

1. Add all of the sauce ingredients into a food processor and blitz until smooth.
2. Heat a wok or large pan over a high heat. When it's hot, add the oil to coat the pan.
3. Add the chicken and cook for 5 minutes.
4. Add the rice and vegetables, mix well and cook for a few minutes.
5. Add the sauce and cook for a further 2 minutes.
6. Finally, mix through the fresh coriander/cilantro, check the seasoning and serve, topped with a scattering of sesame seeds.

Chicken Tenders with Corn Relish

A healthy take on the ever-popular fried chicken. Obviously, it isn't deep fried, but breaded and baked. Served here with a tangy sweetcorn relish.

Serves 3–4

Ingredients:

For the chicken:
  Chicken mini fillets: 454g/1 lb
  Buckwheat or other gluten-free flour: 4 tablespoons
  Eggs: 2, beaten
  Gluten-free breadcrumbs: 100g/3½ oz
  Olive oil: 2 tablespoons
  Butter or dairy-free alternative: 2 tablespoons

For the relish:
  Olive oil: 1 tablespoon
  Onion: 1 small, finely diced
  Sweetcorn/corn: 200g/7 oz can, drained (or fresh)
  Apple cider vinegar: 4 tablespoons
  Caster/superfine sugar: 25g
  Pink Himalayan salt: ½ teaspoon
  English mustard powder: ½ teaspoon
  Fresh lime: Juice of ½
  Fresh coriander/cilantro to garnish

Method:

1. Preheat the oven to 200°C/fan 180°C/400°F/gas mark 6.
2. Season the chicken with salt & pepper.
3. Tip the flour into one bowl, beat the eggs into a separate bowl. Add the breadcrumbs into yet another bowl and you are ready to start.
4. One at a time, dredge the chicken in the flour, shaking off any excess, then dip into the egg, and finally dredge in the breadcrumbs until completely coated.
5. Heat half the butter and oil in a frying pan/skillet over a medium to high heat. Add half of the chicken and cook for 2–3 minutes on each side until golden. Remove and place on a baking tray. Repeat for the remaining chicken and once browned on each side, place in a preheated oven for 5–8 minutes until cooked through.
6. For the relish, heat a pan on the hob over a low heat and add the oil.
7. Add the onion and soften for 10 minutes.
8. After the 10 minutes, add the corn, vinegar, sugar, salt and mustard. Bring to the boil and then reduce the heat. Cook for a few minutes then remove from the heat, add the lime, coriander and cool a little before serving with the chicken and a green salad, sweet potato wedges or polenta chips.

Chicken, Tarragon & Haricot Beans

This is a great dinner, easy to put together and one that combines the classic flavours of chicken and tarragon. The haricot beans really bulk the dish up. Other beans such as butter beans or cannellini beans would work well too.

Serves 2

Ingredients:

    Skinless chicken breasts: 2
    Olive oil: 1 tablespoon
    Chicken stock: 500ml/2 cups
    Haricot beans: 2 x 400g/15 oz can
    Crème fraiche or dairy-free alternative: 1 tablespoon
    Fresh or dried tarragon: 1 tablespoon, chopped
    Flat leaf parsley: 1 tablespoon, chopped

Method:

1. Preheat the oven to 200°C/fan 180°C/400°F/gas mark 6.
2. Heat the oil in an oven safe frying pan/skillet or stock pot on the hob over a medium heat.
3. Season the chicken with salt & pepper and add to the pan and brown for 3 minutes each side.
4. Add the stock, drained beans, tarragon and crème fraiche to the pan and mix well. Cover and transfer to the oven. Cook for 20 minutes.
5. After 20 minutes, check the chicken – it should be cooked through. If so, remove it from the pan and rest for a couple of minutes. Add the chopped

parsley to the beans and mix well. Check you're happy with the seasoning then serve with the chicken and some greens of your choice.

Roast Chicken with Sage & Onion Stuffing Balls

The roast dinner is quintessentially British. I've kept the recipe here to just the chicken, gravy and stuffing because there are a range of additions that can be found in the basics section of this book that would work well with this – Honey roast root vegetables, celeriac mash, Yorkshire puddings…

Serves 4–6

Ingredients:

- Whole chicken: 1, about 1.5kg/3 lb
- Olive oil: 2–3 tablespoons
- Onions: 2, roughly chopped
- Garlic: 4 cloves, crushed
- Bunch of thyme: 1
- Buckwheat or other gluten-free flour: 1 tablespoon
- Red wine: 250ml/1 cup
- Chicken stock: 1 litre/4 cups

For the stuffing:
- Olive oil: 1 tablespoon
- Onion: 1, finely diced
- Fresh sage: 4 sprigs, leaves picked and chopped
- Gluten-free breadcrumbs: 80g/3 oz
- Egg: 1, beaten

Method:

1. Preheat the oven to 200°C/fan 180°C/400°F/gas mark 6.
2. Remove the chicken from the fridge 30 minutes prior to roasting to bring it up to room temperature.
3. Put the onions, garlic and a few of the thyme sprigs into a roasting tray, drizzle with olive oil and season with salt & pepper.
4. Sit the chicken on top of the onions, place the rest of the herbs down the cavity of the chicken, rub some olive oil over the chicken and season with salt & pepper.
5. Cooking times for the chicken will vary depending on its weight. Cook for 20 minutes per 450g, plus 20 minutes extra. Baste the chicken halfway through the cooking time.
6. For the stuffing balls, warm the oil in a frying pan/skillet over a low to medium heat and sweat the onions for 10 minutes. Remove from the heat, season well with salt & pepper and transfer to a mixing bowl. Mix in the onions, sage, breadcrumbs and egg. Shape into balls the size of a golf ball, grease a baking tray and roast in the oven for the final 30 minutes of the chicken.
7. When it's cooked, remove the chicken from the oven and transfer it to a board, cover in foil and rest for 15 minutes.
8. For the gravy, place the roasting tray onto the hob (or transfer to a hob safe pan) and mix the flour into the onions, giving everything a good mash. Turn the heat up and mix in the wine, cook for a couple of minutes to burn off the alcohol, then add the stock. Boil for 10 minutes or so, stirring and mashing as you go.
9. Get another pan out and place a coarse sieve over it. Pour your gravy into it, ensuring that you get as much flavour out of the onions as possible. You should be left with a really flavoursome gravy. Serve with the chicken, stuffing and veg of your choice.

Lamb Ragu

The reason I wanted to add a version of a red meat ragu to the book was due to the universal popularity of it. It has to be one of Italy's best-loved exports around the world, doesn't it? It's versatile too; I've created a recipe that serves 8 portions because I think this is a good dish to make in large quantities for freezing, as there are other dishes you could do with it – shepherd's pie or topping for a pizza/flatbread. The recipe can be easily halved.

Serves 8

Ingredients:

- **Olive oil: 2 tablespoons**
- **Ground/minced lamb: 1kg/2 lb**
- **Onions: 2, finely diced**
- **Celery: 2 sticks, finely diced**
- **Carrots: 2, finely diced**
- **Red wine: 250ml/1 cup**
- **Fresh rosemary: 4 tablespoons**
- **Fresh parsley: 4 tablespoons**
- **Chicken stock: 1 litre/4 cups**

Method:

1. Heat the oil in a large pan/skillet over a moderate heat and add the lamb. Brown all over to seal the meat and break down any clumps. Remove and set aside.
2. Add the onion, carrot, celery and rosemary to the pan, reduce the heat to its lowest setting. Sweat the vegetables for 10 minutes.

3. Add the lamb back to the pan, stir well. Turn up the heat and add the red wine. Reduce until the wine has almost evaporated.
4. Add the stock and cook down for 20 minutes or so.
5. Scatter with parsley and serve with some gluten-free pasta of your choice and a green salad.

Lamb Steak with Butter Bean & Spinach Mash

Such a simple dish to make, it only takes a little time and effort, which is a definite thumbs up from me for a quick mid-week dinner!

Serves 2

Ingredients:

    Lamb leg steaks: 2
    Olive oil: 1 tablespoon
    Butter beans: 2 x 400g/15 oz cans
    Spinach: 2 handfuls
    Chicken stock: 250ml/1 cup
    Crème fraiche or dairy-free alternative: 1 tablespoon
    Rosemary oil: A drizzle (optional)

Method:

1. Preheat the oven to 200°C/fan 180°C/400°F/gas mark 6.
2. Heat a frying pan/skillet over a high heat. Season the lamb with salt & pepper and mix with the olive oil. When the pan is hot, add the lamb and cook for 3 minutes on each side, then finish off in the oven for 5 minutes for a medium finish. Once done, remove and rest for 5 minutes before serving. Cook for longer than the 5 minutes in the oven if you prefer it to be more well done.
3. Whilst the lamb is under way, get to work on the beans. Add the chicken stock to a saucepan on the hob over a medium heat. Rinse the butter beans and add to the stock, along with the spinach. Cook for 5 minutes.

4. After 5 minutes, transfer to a blender (or use a stick blender) and blitz to a smooth puree. Transfer back to the pan, mix in the crème fraiche and season to your liking with salt & pepper.
5. Add the mashed beans to a bowl, top with a piece of the lamb and drizzle with a little rosemary oil if you have some to finish it off. Serve with some greens of your choice.

Lamb, Rosemary & Garlic Meatballs

Pairing lamb with rosemary and garlic is a classic combination. I love making these – you could have them with brown rice or gluten-free pasta, pitta bread or Yorkshire pudding with roasted vegetables.

Serves 4

Ingredients:

    Olive oil: 2 tablespoons
    Onion: 1, finely diced
    Garlic: 2 cloves, minced
    Egg: 1, beaten
    Ground/minced lamb: 450g/1 lb
    Gluten-free breadcrumbs: 100g/3½ oz
    Fresh rosemary: 2 tablespoons, finely chopped
    Fresh parsley: 2 tablespoons, finely chopped
    Pink Himalayan salt: ½ teaspoon

Method:

1. Preheat the oven to 220°C/fan 200°C/425°F/gas mark 7.
2. Heat the oil in a large frying pan/skillet on a low heat and add the onions. Cook for 10 minutes.
3. Add the garlic and cook for another 5 minutes before removing from the heat and allowing to cool down.
4. Beat the egg in a mixing bowl then add all of the remaining ingredients, including the onions and mix well.

5. Form the mixture into 16 balls, each should be about the size of a golf ball. Place them on a baking tray lined with non-stick baking parchment and bake in the oven for 20 minutes and serve.
6. Serve any way you like – I like to have them with onion gravy and some roasted vegetables.

Lamb Kofta Burger with Tzatziki & Polenta Fries

Popular the world over, I had to include a version of burger and fries for the occasions when you want to indulge. You could do sweet potato or root vegetable wedges to accompany the burger, but I really like polenta fries – the recipe for the fries can be found in the basics section.

Serves 4

Ingredients:

- Olive oil: 2 tablespoons
- Onion: 1, finely diced
- Garlic: 1 clove, minced
- Ground coriander: 1 teaspoon
- Ground cumin: 2 teaspoons
- Ground/minced lamb: 450g/1 lb
- Fresh mint: 2 tablespoons, finely chopped
- Fresh parsley: 2 tablespoons, finely chopped
- Pink Himalayan salt: ½ teaspoon

For the tzatziki:
- Cucumber: 1/2, grated
- Dairy-free Greek yoghurt: 250g/1 cup
- Fresh mint: a few sprigs, finely chopped
- Garlic: 1 clove, minced
- Lemon: Juice of half

Method:

1. Heat half of the oil in a frying pan/skillet on a low heat and add the onions, cook for 10 minutes.
2. Add the garlic, ground cumin and ground coriander and cook for another 5 minutes before removing from the heat and allowing to cool down.
3. Add the onion mixture to a mixing bowl with all of the other burger ingredients. Mix well until it is all combined.
4. Form the mixture into 4 patties and allow it to chill for up to 30 minutes if you have the time.
5. Heat the remaining tablespoon of oil in a frying pan/skillet over a medium heat and fry the burgers for about 10–12 minutes on each side until cooked through.
6. For the tzatziki, mix all of the ingredients together and season with salt & pepper.
7. Top the burgers with tzatziki and serve in gluten-free buns with polenta fries or a green salad.

Shoulder Of Lamb with Boulangere Root Vegetables served with Braised Lettuce & Peas

This is such a perfect lazy weekend dinner that's effortless to put together and just requires a slow and low roast. The result is an exceptional one-pot dish. Also, from sitting the lamb on top of the vegetables, all of the meat juices seep into the vegetables during cooking.

Serves 4–6

Ingredients:

Onions: 3, peeled and thinly sliced
Root vegetables: 1.5kg/3 lb, peeled and thinly sliced (mixture of carrots, parsnip, swede/rutabaga or celeriac)
Fresh rosemary: 3 sprigs, leaves picked and finely chopped
Lamb shoulder: 1, about 2kg/4 lb
Fresh garlic: 5 cloves, peeled and halved lengthways
Chicken stock: 750ml/ 3 cups

For the peas:
Butter or dairy-free alternative: 1 tablespoon
Olive oil: 1 tablespoon
Buckwheat or other gluten-free flour: 1 teaspoon
Chicken stock: 300ml/1¼ cup
Frozen peas: 400g/14 oz
Baby gem lettuce: 2, sliced
Lemon: Juice of 1

Method:

1. Preheat the oven to 170°C/fan 150°C/325°F/gas mark 3.
2. In a large mixing bowl, mix the onions, root vegetables and rosemary. Season with salt & pepper.
3. Layer the vegetable mixture in baking dish at least 30cm x 20cm and place the lamb skin side up.
4. Cut 10 incisions into the lamb, big enough to act as a pocket for the garlic cloves and push the cloves completely into the incisions.
5. Pour over the chicken stock and bake for 4 hours or until the vegetables are crispy on top and cooked through. Check from time to time to make sure that it doesn't dry out. If it looks like it is, add more stock.
6. When the time is up, remove the baking dish from the oven, cover with foil and rest for 20 minutes.
7. While the lamb is resting, make the peas.
8. Heat the butter and oil in a large saucepan over a moderate heat. Add the flour and mix well, then gradually add the stock, stirring constantly. Add the peas and lettuce, season with salt & pepper then simmer for 5 minutes. Finish off with the lemon juice.
9. Serve the peas with the lamb and root vegetables.

Shepherd's Pie with a Root Vegetable Topping

A British classic given a makeover to avoid the white potatoes that usually cover the filling like a thick blanket. It doesn't feel like a compromise either, as the root vegetables do a fine job in standing in for the traditional mash.

Serves 3–4

Ingredients:

    Olive oil: 1 tablespoon
    Ground/minced lamb: 450g/1 lb
    Onion: 1, finely diced
    Celery: 1 stick, finely diced
    Carrot: 1, finely diced
    Garlic: 1 clove, minced
    Fresh rosemary: 1 tablespoon
    Red wine: 125ml/1/2 cup
    Chicken stock: 500ml/2 cups

For the topping:
    Root vegetables: 1kg/2 lb (Mixture of carrots, celeriac, parsnip or swede/rutabaga)
    Extra virgin olive oil: 2 tablespoons

Method:

1. Preheat the oven to 200°C/fan 180°C/400°F/gas mark 6.
2. Heat the oil in a frying pan/skillet over a moderate heat and add the lamb. Brown all over to seal the meat and break down any clumps. Remove and set aside.
3. Add the onion, carrot, celery, rosemary and reduce the heat to its lowest setting. Sweat the vegetables for 15 minutes, adding the garlic after the first 10 minutes.
4. Add the lamb back to the pan and stir well. Turn up the heat and add the red wine. Reduce until the wine has almost evaporated.
5. Add the stock and cook for 20 minutes until it has thickened and reduced. Check the seasoning then place in a baking dish and allow to cool.
6. For the topping, put the veg in a large pan of salted boiling water and boil for 20–25 minutes until tender.
7. Drain in a colander and allow to steam dry for 5 minutes before placing back in the pan and mashing, adding the oil as you do. Mash until smooth and season with salt & pepper.
8. Allow the mash to cool; this should prevent it from sinking into the meat during cooking. Once cool, place on top of the meat and bake for 30–40 minutes until golden brown on top. Serve with some greens of your choice.

Lamb Chilli

I know the title suggests that this is a chilli, but I can assure you that the nightshade has been omitted. However, I have still included the other spices that form the DNA of a Mexican dish that is adored the world over. The lamb serves to replace the beef version that is universally popular.

Serves 3–4

Ingredients:

    Olive oil: 2 tablespoons
    Ground lamb: 454g/1 lb
    Onion: 1, finely diced
    Celery: 1 stick, finely diced
    Carrots: 1, finely diced
    Fresh garlic: 1 clove, minced
    Cinnamon stick: 1
    Ground cumin: 2 teaspoons
    Ground cloves: 2 teaspoons
    Dried oregano: 2 teaspoons
    Red wine: 125ml/1/2 cup
    Vegetable stock: 1 litre/4 cups
    Red kidney beans: 1 x 400g/15 oz can

Method:

1. Heat half of the oil in a large pan/skillet over a moderate heat and add the lamb. Brown all over to seal the meat and break down any clumps. Remove and set aside.

2. Heat the remaining oil in the pan and add the onion, carrot and celery. Sweat the vegetables for 15 minutes. Add the garlic and all of the spices and cook for another 5 minutes.
3. Add the lamb back to the pan, turn up the heat and add the red wine. Reduce until the wine has almost evaporated.
4. Add the stock, beans and cook down for 20 minutes or so, until the flavours are combined, and the stock has reduced.
5. Check the seasoning, adding more salt & pepper to taste and then serve with some brown rice, green salad and a scattering of fresh coriander/cilantro.

Lamb Leg Steak with Tabbouleh & Tahini Sauce

The main thing I like about tabbouleh is that the herbs take a more center role than just being a garnish. A big bunch of parsley and mint add such an element of freshness to this dish.

Serves 4

Ingredients:

    For the lamb:
Lamb leg steaks: 4, boneless
Olive oil: 1 tablespoon

For the tabbouleh:
    Bulgur wheat: 100g/3½ oz
    Fresh parsley: 1 large bunch, chopped
    Fresh mint: 1 small bunch, leaves picked, chopped
    Cucumber: Half, sliced
    Radish: 4, finely sliced
    Spring onions: A bunch, finely sliced
    Fresh lemon: 1, juice only
    Extra virgin olive oil: 4 tbsp
    Pomegranate: 1, seeds removed

Tahini sauce:
    Tahini: 80g/3 oz
    Lemon juice: 2 tablespoons
    Garlic: 1 clove, minced

Method:

1. For the tabbouleh, cook the bulgur wheat according to the packet instructions and allow to cool completely. When cooled, add to a large mixing bowl along with the fresh parsley, mint, chopped cucumber, radish, spring onions and then mix in the lemon juice and olive oil. Season with salt & pepper and finally mix in the pomegranate seeds.
2. For the lamb, heat a frying or griddle pan over a high heat. When the pan is hot, add the lamb and cook for 3–5 minutes on each side, depending on how you like your lamb cooked.
3. For the tahini sauce, whisk all of the ingredients together in a bowl and gradually add in some ice-cold water until smooth and at a consistency that isn't too thick. Season with salt.
4. To serve, add a portion of the tabbouleh to a bowl and top with the lamb chops and a drizzle of the tahini sauce.

Lamb Henry

When I was 18, I moved to the Lake District in the UK and found a job as a waiter in a hotel. One of the most popular dishes served there was a dish called Lamb Henry. I'd never heard of it before but found myself serving it on a daily basis, due to its unwavering popularity. And what was it? Lamb shank braised in garlic and rosemary, slow cooked until the meat is just about to give way and fall off the bone, served on a bed of buttery mashed potato and finished with a reduction of its own cooking liquor. No wonder it was so popular.

Serves 4

Ingredients:

For the lamb:
Lamb shanks: 4
Olive oil: 2 tablespoons
Onion: 1, diced
Celery: 1 stick, chopped
Carrot: 1, chopped
Fresh garlic: 4 cloves, chopped
Red wine: 250ml/1 cup
Chicken stock: 1 litre/4 cups

For the mash:
Mixed root vegetables of your choice (I like using carrots, swede/rutabaga, sweet potato and parsnip): 1kg/2 lb, chopped
Butter or dairy-free alternative: 25g/1 oz
Fresh chives: 3 tablespoons

Method:

1. Preheat the oven to 170°C/fan 150°C/325°F/gas mark 3.
2. Heat the oil on the hob in a deep casserole dish over a medium to high heat. Season the lamb portions and add to the dish to seal the meat. Turn every few minutes until the lamb is completely sealed and beginning to caramelise. Remove and set aside. Lower the heat to low/medium and add the onion, celery, carrot and rosemary. Cook for 10 minutes, then add the garlic and cook for a further 5 minutes.
3. Turn the heat up and add the red wine. Cook for a couple of minutes to give the alcohol time to evaporate, then add the chicken stock and the lamb portions back to the dish.
4. Cover and place into the oven and cook for 1.5–2 hours. The length of time it takes to cook will vary depending on the meat so start checking it after it's had 1.5 hours. If the lamb is falling away from the bone, it's ready. If not, stick it back in the oven for another 30 minutes before checking again. When ready, remove the lamb from the dish, cover the meat with foil and let it rest.
5. To make the gravy, place the dish the lamb was in onto the hob and cook over a high heat for 10 minutes to reduce and to mash the veg up, then pass through a sieve into another pan. Now, depending on how thick the sauce is, you can either reduce it further on the hob, or if you're happy with it, leave it to simmer over a low heat, adding the lamb back to it.
6. Boil the root vegetables in salted water until soft. Drain and allow to steam off for a couple of minutes to dry out a little. Then mash until smooth, mix in the butter, chives and season with salt & pepper. Serve the mash in the middle of the plate, placing the lamb on top along with a ladle full of the cooking liquor.

Lamb & Chickpea Saag

This is a slow cooked lamb curry without the usual ingredients of tomato and chilli. What you're left with is something very fragrant with a much milder spice to it. If you're a curry lover, this is a nightshade free curry to add to your repertoire.

Serves 3–4

Ingredients:

    Olive oil: 3 tablespoons
    Diced lamb leg: 450g/1 lb
    Onions: 2, sliced
    Garlic: 2 cloves, minced
    Cardamom pods: 6, seeds only
    Coriander seeds: 2 teaspoons
    Cumin seeds: 2 teaspoons
    Yellow mustard seeds: 1 teaspoon
    Ground cinnamon: 1 teaspoon
    Ground turmeric: 1 teaspoon
    Spinach: 250g/9 oz
    Chicken stock: 500ml/2 cups
    Chick peas: 1 x 400g/15 oz can

Method:

1. Preheat the oven to 190°C/fan 170°C/375°F/gas mark 5.
2. Heat 1 tablespoon of the oil in a deep casserole dish on the hob over a medium heat, preferably one that's oven safe and has a lid. Season the

lamb with salt & pepper and add to the pan to seal. Cook for 5 minutes or so until completely browned, then remove the lamb from the pan and set aside.

3. Reduce the heat, add the remaining oil and the onions. Cook for 15 minutes then add the garlic and cook for a further 5 minutes.
4. Whilst the onions are cooking, you need to get the spices together. Heat a dry frying pan over a high heat and add the cardamom seeds, coriander seeds, cumin seeds and mustard seeds. Toast for 2–3 minutes without burning until fragrant, then remove and place in a pestle & mortar and grind until it's a fine powder.
5. After the onion and garlic have had 20 minutes, add the spices you've just ground, along with the other ground spices (cinnamon and turmeric). Cook for a couple more minutes to give everything a good mix. Then add half of the spinach and cook for a few minutes until it starts to wilt.
6. Remove the mixture from the pan and transfer to a food processor and blend until it resembles a smooth paste. Transfer back to the pan along with the lamb and 500ml of chicken stock. Season with salt & pepper and bring to the boil.
7. When it is boiling, place a lid onto it and transfer to the oven for 2 hours or until the lamb is tender. 20 minutes before the cooking time is up, add in the chickpeas and spinach.
8. When cooked, serve with a scattering of fresh coriander/cilantro and yoghurt along with some brown rice.

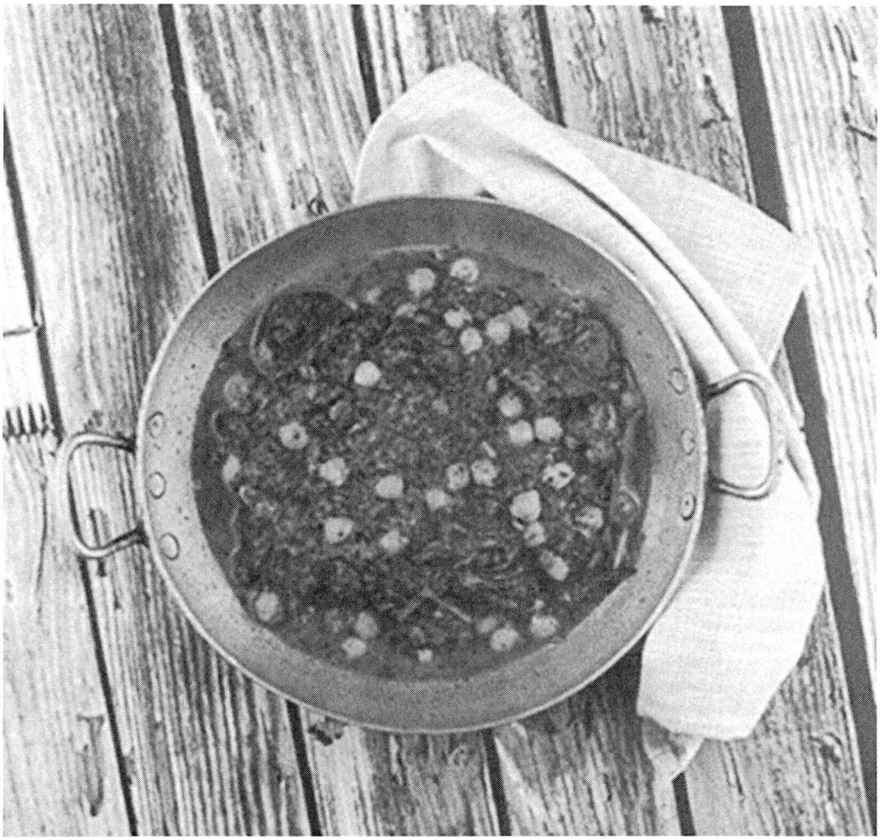

Tamari & Honey Turkey Stir Fry

This marinade is great for taking a plain piece of turkey and transforming it into something much more appealing. The addition of honey gives it a great sweetness and stickiness too. Feel free to adapt the vegetables to whatever you have to hand. For the rice, either use precooked brown rice pouches or boil some ahead of cooking.

Serves 2

Ingredients:

> For the turkey:
> Turkey breast steaks: 2, about 150g/5 oz per steak
> Honey: 1 tablespoon
> Tamari: 1 tablespoon
> Sesame oil: 1 tablespoon
> Fresh garlic: 1 clove, minced
> Fresh ginger: 1 teaspoon, minced
> For the stir fry
> Olive oil: 2 tablespoons
> Cooked brown basmati rice: 250g/9 oz (or from raw 80g/3 oz)
> Pak choy: 1, leaves cut from the stem
> Asparagus: 1 small bunch, chopped
> Beansprouts: 1 handful
> Fresh coriander/cilantro: Handful, finely chopped
> White & black sesame seeds: 1 teaspoon of each to garnish

Method:

1. Mix all of the marinade ingredients together and add half of it to the turkey. Cover and leave in the fridge for at least 30 minutes. Keep the other half as a sauce for the stir fry.
2. Heat a frying pan/skillet on the hob over a medium heat. Add the turkey and cook on each side for 5 minutes until cooked through.
3. Meanwhile, heat a wok or large pan. When it's hot, add the oil to coat the pan.
4. Add the asparagus, rice, beansprouts and reserved marinade. Mix well and cook for a couple of minutes.
5. Add the pak choy and cook for another few minutes.
6. Finally, mix through the fresh coriander/cilantro and serve, topped with the turkey breast and scattering of some sesame seeds.

Turkey, Lemon Zest & Sage Meatloaf

When I was testing this recipe, I was pleasantly surprised with how it retained its moisture when baked. It's also very easy to make and is quite versatile once cooked – I like it with salad, in a sandwich or with colcannon and spinach.

Serves 4

Ingredients:

    Olive oil: 2 tablespoons
    Onion: 1, finely diced
    Garlic: 2 cloves, minced
    Eggs: 1, beaten
    Ground/minced turkey: 450g/1 lb
    Gluten-free breadcrumbs: 100g/3½ oz
    Dried or fresh sage: 1 tablespoon
    Fresh parsley: 2 tablespoons
    Lemon: 1, zest only
    Pink Himalayan salt: ½ teaspoon

Method:

1. Preheat the oven to 200°C/fan 180°C/400°F/gas mark 6.
2. Heat the oil in a frying pan/skillet on the hob over a low heat and add the onion. Cook for 10 minutes, stirring every now and then. Add the crushed garlic, sage and cook for another 10 minutes until the onion is translucent. Set aside to cool.

3. Beat the egg in a large mixing bowl, then add rest of the ingredients including the onions and mix well with your hands until all is combined.
4. Transfer the mixture to a 1 lb loaf tin and cook in the oven for 40–45 minutes until the top is nice and crispy and it's cooked throughout.

Turkey Schnitzalese

Milanese and schnitzel – There's not much difference between either of them and they both sound a lot better than 'breaded meat'. This recipe is great for turning a simple, lean piece of turkey into a flavourful, savoury, crispy piece of meat. Serve with a salad of your choice, or even some kale colcannon, which is quite similar to how a traditional schnitzel is served as it usually comes with mashed potato.

Serves 4

Ingredients:

    Turkey breast steaks: 4 (approx. 150g/5 oz each)
    Buckwheat or other gluten-free flour: 4 tablespoons
    Garlic salt: 1 teaspoon
    Eggs: 2, beaten
    Gluten-free breadcrumbs: 100g/3½ oz
    Olive oil: 2 tablespoons
    Butter or dairy-free alternative: 2 tablespoons

Method:

1. Preheat the oven to 200°C/fan 180°C/400°F/gas mark 6.
2. Season the turkey with salt & pepper.
3. Tip the flour into one bowl and add the garlic salt. Beat the eggs into a separate bowl. Add the breadcrumbs into yet another bowl and you're ready to start.

4. One at a time, dredge the turkey in the flour, shake off any excess, then dip into the egg before finally dredging in the breadcrumbs until completely coated.
5. Heat half of the butter and oil in a frying pan/skillet over a medium to high heat. Add two steaks and cook for 2–3 minutes on each side until golden. Remove and place on a baking tray. Repeat for the remaining steaks and once browned on each side, place in a preheated oven for 5–8 minutes until cooked through. Serve with a green salad.

Courgette & Turkey Burgers

This is a great alternative to a red meat burger, much leaner and the addition of courgette/zucchini gives it a fresh taste. The recipe can be easily halved.

Serves 6

Ingredients:

    Ground/minced turkey: 450g/1 lb
    Grated courgette/zucchini: 450g/1 lb
    Dried oregano: 2 tablespoons
    Bicarbonate of soda: 2 teaspoons
    Pink Himalayan salt: ½ teaspoon
    Olive oil: 1 tablespoon
    Gluten-free buns: 6
    Rocket/arugula: a handful

Method:

1. Squeeze out as much moisture as you can from the grated courgette/zucchini and add it to a mixing bowl with the turkey, herbs, bicarbonate of soda, salt, a good twist of black pepper. Mix all of the ingredients until well combined. Split into 6 even sizes and shape into burgers. Cover and chill in the fridge for 30 minutes.
2. Preheat the oven to 220°C/fan 200°C/425°F/gas mark 7.
3. Heat a frying pan/skillet on a medium heat and add the olive oil. Fry the burgers for 2–3 minutes on each side to give them a bit of colour then transfer to the oven and cook for 15 minutes.

4. After 15 minutes in the oven, the burgers should be cooked. Check the temperature of them to make sure. If they are not quite cooked, put them back in the oven for a few minutes.
5. When cooked, serve in the buns topped with rocket/arugula and vegan mayonnaise.

Turkey & Almond Satay Noodles

I've been a fan of satay for years; a bold sauce that sticks to the roof of your mouth when you eat it. Here I've changed the usual peanut butter for almond butter as it is less acidic. Although milder in taste, it still works in this sauce.

Serves 2

Ingredients:

For the satay:
- Spring onions/scallions: 4, trimmed and sliced
- Fresh lime: juice of ½
- Tamari: 1 tablespoon
- Fresh coriander/cilantro: 1 tablespoon
- Almond butter: 1 tablespoon
- Garlic: 1 clove, minced
- Ginger: A thumb sized piece, minced
- Ground cumin: ¼ teaspoon
- Ground turmeric: ¼ teaspoon
- Water: 1 tablespoon

For the rest:
- Olive oil: 1 tablespoon
- Ground/minced turkey: 200g/7 oz
- Dried rice noodles: 100g/3½ oz
- Asparagus: A bunch, sliced
- Spinach: A handful
- Frozen peas: A handful

Method:

1. Add all of the sauce ingredients into a food processor and blitz until smooth.
2. Cook the noodles according to the packet instructions and set aside.
3. Heat a wok or large pan. When it's hot, add the oil to coat the pan.
4. Add the turkey to the pan and cook for 5 minutes until it is well-sealed and beginning to colour.
5. Add the asparagus and stir fry for 5 minutes.
6. Add the peas, noodles, sauce and stir fry for a couple of minutes until everything is mixed well.
7. Add the spinach and cook for another minute, until it starts to wilt.
8. Finally, mix through some fresh coriander/cilantro and serve.

Vegetables

Pea & Mint Risotto

Brown rice offers a great alternative to the usual white rice used in a risotto. The flavours in this dish make for a perfect spring dish.

Serves 3–4

Ingredients:

    Olive oil: 2 tablespoons
    Onion: 1, finely chopped
    Celery: 1 stick, finely chopped
    Garlic: 2 cloves, minced
    Brown rice: 200g/7 oz
    Vegetable stock: 1 litre/4 cups
    Frozen peas: 150g/5 oz
    Courgette/zucchini: 2, sliced
    Fresh mint: 3 sprigs, leaves picked, finely chopped
    Lemon: Juice of ½

Method:

1. Heat half of the oil in a large saucepan over a low heat, add the onion and celery. Cook for 10 minutes, add the garlic and cook for another 5 minutes.
2. Stir in the rice for a minute, then add the stock to the pan and bring to the boil. Simmer for 30 minutes, stirring occasionally.
3. After 30 minutes check on the rice and if necessary, add more stock and cook for another 5–10 minutes. When it's almost done, add the peas and cook for 5 minutes.

4. While the risotto is cooking, get a griddle pan on a medium heat. Mix the sliced courgette/zucchini with some olive oil and season with salt & pepper. Place on the griddle pan and cook for 2–3 minutes on each side until charred. Set aside.
5. To finish off, add the courgette/zucchini to the risotto, along with the lemon juice and mint. Give it a stir and check the seasoning, adding more salt & pepper if required.

Roast Cauliflower with Tahini & Pomegranate

Roasting cauliflower is a great way to cook this much underrated vegetable. It takes on a smoky, more intense flavour, which works perfectly with the spice mix that it's smothered in. Dressed with pomegranate, pine nuts and tahini, it's also a very vibrant plate when served.

Serves 2–3

Ingredients:

Cauliflower: 1, leaves removed
Cauliflower spice mix:
Olive oil: 3 tablespoons
Lemon: Juice of 1
Garlic: 1 clove, minced
Fresh coriander: 2 tablespoons
Ground cinnamon: 1 tablespoon
Sumac: 1 tablespoon
Ground cumin: 1½ teaspoons
Ground cloves: ½ teaspoon
Nutmeg: A light grating
Pink Himalayan salt: ½ teaspoon
Tahini sauce:
Tahini: 80g/3 oz
Lemon juice: 2 tablespoons
Garlic: 1 clove, minced

To garnish:
Pomegranate seeds: 3 tablespoons
Pine nuts: 2 tablespoons, toasted

Method:

1. Preheat the oven to 200°C/fan 180°C/400°F/gas mark 6.
2. Bring a large pot of salted water to the boil on the hob and boil the whole cauliflower for 8 minutes.
3. After 8 minutes, remove the cauliflower, place onto a baking dish and allow to steam dry for a couple of minutes.
4. Mix all of the spice mix together and then brush the mix over the cauliflower. Place in a preheated oven and roast for 30–40 minutes until nicely charred.
5. For the tahini sauce, whisk all of the ingredients together in a bowl and gradually add in some ice-cold water until smooth and at a consistency that isn't too thick. Season with salt.
6. When the cauliflower is cooked, remove from the oven and place onto a serving dish, scatter the pomegranate seeds, pine nuts and drizzle the tahini sauce over it. Serve with a green salad and some quinoa.

Pasta with Spinach Balls & a Courgette & Kale Sauce

This is a recipe that I've adapted from one that I came across in an Italian restaurant. That recipe featured a lot of chilli, which has been omitted, opting instead for a milder sauce.

Serves 2

Ingredients:

For the spinach balls:
    Spinach: 250g/9 oz
    Egg: 1, beaten
    Garlic: 1 clove, minced
    Gluten-free breadcrumbs: 50g/2 oz
    Nutmeg: A light grating
    Olive oil: 1 tablespoon

For the pasta:
    Gluten-free pasta: 200g
    Olive oil: 2 tablespoons
    Garlic: 2 cloves, minced
    Courgettes: 1, sliced
    Kale: 100g/3½ oz, chopped
    Toasted pine nuts: 2 tablespoons

Method:

1. For the spinach balls, add the spinach to a pan of salted boiling water and cook for 2 minutes, then drain thoroughly, squeezing out as much water as you can.
2. Chop the spinach and then add to a mixing bowl with the egg, garlic, breadcrumbs, nutmeg and some salt & pepper. Mix well and then shape into ping pong sized balls.
3. Heat the oil in a frying pan/skillet on the hob over a medium heat. Fry the spinach balls for 5 minutes or until cooked and golden all over.
4. Whilst the spinach is underway, boil the pasta according to the packet instructions and make the sauce.
5. For the sauce, heat the oil in a frying pan/skillet over a medium heat, then add the garlic, kale, courgette, salt & pepper and fry for 5–7 minutes or so, until the vegetables are just about cooked. At this point, mix in the drained pasta, along with a few tablespoons of pasta water to loosen the sauce up. Check the seasoning, then serve topped with the spinach balls and some toasted pine nuts.

Puy Lentil, Butternut Squash & Spinach Stew

Lentils are a great vehicle for flavour, especially puy lentils that seem to hold their shape better than other varieties. Because of lentils having the propensity to take on other flavours, this dish works in a similar way to a risotto, minus the endless stirring.

Serves 3–4

Ingredients:

- **Olive oil: 2 tablespoons**
- **Onions: 1, finely chopped**
- **Fresh garlic: 1 clove, minced**
- **Fresh thyme: 2 sprigs, leaves picked**
- **Puy lentils: 200g/7 oz**
- **Vegetable stock: 750ml/3 cups**
- **Butternut squash: 1 medium sized, peeled and chopped into 2cm pieces**
- **Parsley: 1 handful, chopped**
- **Dairy-free crème fraiche: 2 tablespoons**
- **Spinach: 100g/3½ oz**

Method:

1. For the squash, preheat the oven to 200°C/fan 180°C/400°F/gas mark 6. Mix the squash with half of the oil, season with salt & pepper and roast for 30 minutes until cooked.

2. While the squash is underway, heat the remaining oil in a large pot on the hob over a gentle heat and sweat the onions for 10 minutes, then add the garlic, thyme and fry for another 5 minutes.
3. Add the lentils and give them a good coating, in the same way you would when making a risotto.
4. Add 500ml of the stock and mix well. Simmer for 30–40 minutes or until the lentils are cooked, adding more stock if it begins to dry out.
5. Finally, mix in the squash, crème fraiche and parsley; check the seasoning adding salt & pepper to taste.
6. Serve in bowls with some crusty gluten-free bread for a warming supper.

Butternut Squash, Sage & Red Onion Pasta Topped with Pangrattato

This is quite a moreish pasta dish and easy to put together. Simply roast the vegetables and then mix in with the pasta, crème fraiche and parmesan to form a sauce.

Serves 3–4

Ingredients:

Olive oil: 2 tablespoons
Butternut squash: 1 medium, peeled and cut into 2cm squares
Red onion: 2, peeled and cut into wedges
Dried sage: 1 teaspoon
Gluten-free pasta: 300g/10½ oz
Dairy-free crème fraiche: 2 tablespoons
Vegan parmesan: 50g/2 oz, grated (optional)

For the pangrattato:
Olive oil: 1 tablespoon
Gluten-free breadcrumbs: 1 handful
Fresh parsley: 2 tablespoons
Garlic: 1 clove, minced

Method:

1. Preheat the oven to 200°C/fan 180°C/400°F/gas mark 6.
2. Add the squash, onion, sage, salt & pepper to a baking dish (approx. 30cm x 20cm) along with the oil. Give everything a good mix and place in the preheated oven for 30 minutes or until cooked, giving it a good mix halfway through.
3. In the last 15 minutes of cooking, add the pasta to a pan of salted boiling water and cook according to the packet instructions.
4. Heat a separate frying pan/skillet over a moderate heat and when it's hot, add the oil, garlic and breadcrumbs. Heat for a few minutes, until the breadcrumbs turn golden, then add the parsley and some salt & pepper. Continue to cook for a minute, being careful not to burn the breadcrumbs. Remove from the heat and set aside.
5. When the pasta is cooked, drain, reserving a cup of the pasta water. Take the squash out of the oven once it's cooked and add the pasta to it, along with the crème fraiche and the parmesan. Give everything a good mix, adding a little pasta water to loosen it all up.
6. Serve in bowls, topped with pangrattato.

Puy Lentil Shepherd's Pie with a Sweet Potato Topping

This is a great vegetarian alternative to a British classic. It is versatile too, make 2–3 times the quantity of the lentil mixture and you can portion and freeze it, to be used for other meals.

Serves 4

Ingredients:

    Olive oil: 2 tablespoons
    Onion: 1, finely chopped
    Carrot: 1, finely chopped
    Celery: 1 stick, finely chopped
    Leek: 1, finely chopped
    Garlic: 2 cloves, minced
    Rosemary: 1 sprig, chopped
    Red wine; 125 ml/1/2 cup
    Puy lentils: 200g/7 oz
    Vegetable stock: 750 ml/3 cups

For the mash:
    Sweet potatoes: 1kg/2 lb
    Butter or dairy-free alternative: 2 tablespoons

Method:

1. Preheat the oven to 200°C/fan 180°C/400°F/gas mark 6.
2. Heat the oil in a large pot on the hob over a low heat and add the onion, carrot, celery, leek and rosemary. Sweat the vegetables for 15 minutes, adding the garlic after the first 10 minutes.
3. Add the lentils and give everything a good mix before adding the red wine and reducing for a couple of minutes.
4. Add the stock, cover and cook down for 30 minutes or so, until the lentils are cooked. Check the seasoning then remove from the hob and place in a baking dish and allow to cool.
5. For the topping, put the sweet potatoes in a large pan of salted boiling water and boil for 15–20 minutes.
6. Drain in a colander and allow to steam dry for 5 minutes before placing back in the pan and mashing, adding the butter as you do. Mash until smooth and season with salt & pepper.
7. Allow the mash to cool; this should prevent it from sinking into the filling during cooking. Once cool, place on top of the filling and bake for 30 minutes until golden brown.

Sweet Potato Gnocchi with Almond Pesto

This is a great alternative to the white potato variety, you just need to make sure that you add enough flour to dry the potato out enough to form it into dumplings. If you don't want to make them with parmesan simply replace with extra flour.

Serves 2

Ingredients:

    For the gnocchi:
    Sweet potato: Enough for 300g/10½ oz when cooked and skinned
    Vegan parmesan: 50g/2 oz
    Buckwheat or other gluten-free flour: 100g/3½ oz
    Olive oil: 1 tablespoon
    Butter or dairy-free alternative: 1 tablespoon

    For the pesto: See basics section

Method:

1. Preheat the oven to 220°C/fan 200°C/425°F/gas mark 7.
2. Bake the whole sweet potatoes for an hour, then remove from the oven and allow to cool.
3. Cut the potato in half and scoop out the flesh. If you have one, pass through a potato ricer, if not, mash the potatoes until smooth and free of any lumps. Add the potato to a bowl along with the parmesan and most of the flour. Season and mix well. The correct consistency to have is one

that is like a soft pliable dough, so if it's a bit wet, add some more flour until you have the right consistency.

4. Take half of the mix out onto a floured surface and roll it out into a long strip, the thickness of your thumb. Cut the strip into individual gnocchi, about 3cm each, then press against the back of a fork. Repeat this process with the remaining dough.
5. Bring a large pan of salted water to the boil and cook the gnocchi in batches. When they float to the surface, they're ready. Remove, drain and set aside whilst you cook the rest.
6. Heat a large frying pan/skillet over a medium to high heat and add the olive oil and butter. Add the gnocchi to the pan and fry for 3–5 minutes on each side until golden brown.
7. Serve the gnocchi with some almond pesto from the basics section and some rocket/arugula.

Black Bean 'Chilli'

I know the title suggests that this is a chilli, but I can assure you that the nightshade has been omitted. However, I've still included the other spices that form the DNA of a Mexican dish that is adored the world over.

Serves 3–4

Ingredients:

    Olive oil: 2 tablespoons
    Onion: 1, finely diced
    Celery: 1 stick, finely diced
    Carrot: 1, finely diced
    Fresh garlic: 2 cloves, minced
    Cinnamon stick: 1
    Ground cumin: 2 teaspoons
    Ground cloves: 2 teaspoons
    Dried oregano: 2 teaspoons
    Red wine: 125ml/1/2 cup
    Vegetable stock: 1 litre/4 cups
    Black beans: 2 x 400g/15 oz can

Method:

1. Heat the oil in a large pan/skillet over a moderate heat and add the onion, carrot, celery and reduce the heat to its lowest setting. Sweat the vegetables for 10 minutes. Add the garlic, all of the spices and cook for another 5 minutes.

2. Turn up the heat and add the red wine. Reduce until the wine has almost evaporated.
3. Add the stock, beans and cook for 20 minutes or so.
4. Check the seasoning, adding more salt & pepper to taste and then serve with some brown rice.

Puy Lentil & Mushroom Ragu

Ragu is one of Italy's most popular exports, enjoyed the world over! As a vegetarian alternative, I've used puy lentils and mushrooms. What really stands out in this dish is the use of the beetroot sauce, which is such a great alternative to using tomatoes, the recipe for it can be found in the basics section of this book.

Serves 3–4

Ingredients:

Olive oil: 2 tablespoons
Onion: 1, chopped
Carrot: 1, chopped
Celery: 1 stick, chopped
Garlic: 2 cloves, minced
Rosemary: 1 sprig, chopped
Chestnut mushrooms: 200g/7 oz
Puy lentils: 100g/3½ oz
Beetroot sauce: 250ml/1 cup
Vegetable stock: 500ml/2 cups

Method:

1. Heat the oil in a large pot on the hob over a gentle heat and sweat the onion, carrot and celery for 10 minutes. Season with salt & pepper then add the garlic, mushrooms, rosemary and fry for another 5 minutes.
2. Add the lentils and mix well for a minute, then add the beetroot sauce, stock and mix well.

3. Bring to the boil then reduce to a low heat and simmer for 30 minutes or until the lentils are cooked. If at any point it looks a bit dry, top up with water. When the lentils are cooked, check the seasoning, adding any salt & pepper if necessary. Serve with gluten-free pasta of your choice.

Sweet Potato & Black Bean Vegballs

Versatile, very filling and comforting, this vegball mix can also be used as a burger, with a salad, pasta, rice or in a sandwich.

Serves 3–4

Ingredients:

- **Olive oil:** 2 tablespoons
- **Sweet potato:** 400g/14 oz, peeled and cut into chunks
- **Onion:** 1, chopped
- **Cooked brown rice:** 250g/9 oz pouch (or boil 80g/3 oz dry brown rice)
- **Gluten-free breadcrumbs:** 25g/1 oz
- **Pink Himalayan salt:** ½ teaspoon
- **Black pepper:** ½ teaspoon
- **Ground cumin:** 1 teaspoon
- **Garlic powder:** ½ teaspoon
- **Black beans:** 1 x 400g/15 oz can
- **Fresh coriander/cilantro:** A handful

Method:

1. Preheat the oven to 200°C/fan 180°C/400°F/gas mark 6.
2. Place the sweet potato and 1 tablespoon of olive oil onto a baking tray and roast for 30–40 minutes until cooked. After this time, remove and allow to cool a little.

3. Heat another tablespoon of oil in a frying pan/skillet over a gentle heat and sweat the onion for 10 minutes. Then remove and add to a mixing bowl with all of the other ingredients, including the sweet potato.
4. Blitz everything together with a stick blender until combined, then shape into 12 balls.
5. Grease a baking tray, then add the balls to it and bake for 20 minutes until crisp and golden. Serve with some salad, pasta, rice or in a sandwich.

Sweet

Vanilla Jelly

Like a panna cotta, yet fewer calories. Much fewer actually, but that definitely works in your favour as it's guilt-free.

Serves 4

Ingredients:

> **Leaf gelatine: 4 sheets**
> **Dairy-free milk: 600ml/2½ cups**
> **Caster/superfine sugar: 50g/2 oz**
> **Vanilla paste: 2 teaspoons**
> **Raspberries: 200g/7 oz**

Method:

1. Soak the gelatine for 10 minutes in enough cold water to cover the leaves.
2. Bring the milk and sugar slowly to the boil in a saucepan, gently stirring to dissolve the sugar. Remove from the heat and stir in the vanilla extract.
3. Remove the gelatine from the soaking water, squeezing out any excess water, then stir into the milk until dissolved. Pour the mix into 4 moulds or ramekins. Cool, then chill until set, which should take about 3 hours.
4. To serve the jellies, carefully tip them out onto individual plates and scatter some raspberries around them.

Fresh Fruit Salad with an Orange & Vanilla Syrup

A big bowl of fresh fruit salad is a very colourful and inviting sight. Elevated with an orange and vanilla syrup and it moves into another level. Quick to throw together and very refreshing.

Serves 4

Ingredients:

    Granulated sugar: ¼ cup
    Water: ¼ cup
    Orange: Zest & juice of ½
    Vanilla extract or paste: ½ teaspoon
    Mixed fresh fruit of your choice: 900g/ 2lb
    Mint leaves: A few to garnish

Methd:

1. Add the sugar, water, vanilla, orange juice and zest to a small saucepan and stir. Bring to the boil, then turn down the heat to a low simmer for 10 minutes or until thickened.
2. After the 10 minutes, set aside and cool.
3. Mix the fruit together in a bowl, add the syrup and combine. Garnish with mint and serve.

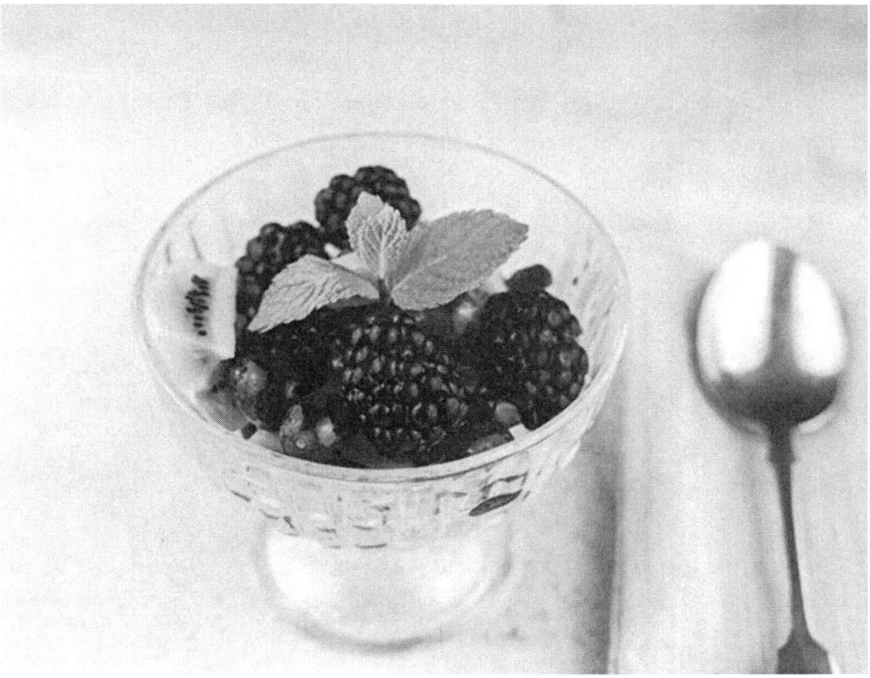

Apple Crumble

Although raw apples are to be eaten alone, cooked apples are fine to be eaten with other ingredients, so here's an apple crumble for those times when some comfort food is required.

Serves 4

Ingredients:

    Apples: 800g/26 oz, peeled, cored and chopped into 2cm pieces
    Caster/superfine sugar: 100g/3 oz
    Buckwheat or other gluten-free flour: 70g/2 oz
    Gluten-free oats: 70g/2 oz
    Unsalted butter or dairy-free alternative: 70g/2 oz

Method:

1. Preheat the oven to 200°C/fan 180°C/400°F/gas mark 6.
2. Add the apples and 50g of the sugar to a saucepan on the hob over a medium heat.
3. Mix well and cook for 5–10 minutes until the apples have softened. When they do, remove from the heat and put to one side.
4. For the topping, rub the butter and flour together in a bowl until it resembles breadcrumbs. Mix in the remaining sugar and the oats.
5. Place the apple mix into a baking dish and sprinkle over the crumble topping.
6. Bake for 25–30 minutes or until golden. Serve with some yoghurt or low-fat custard on the side.

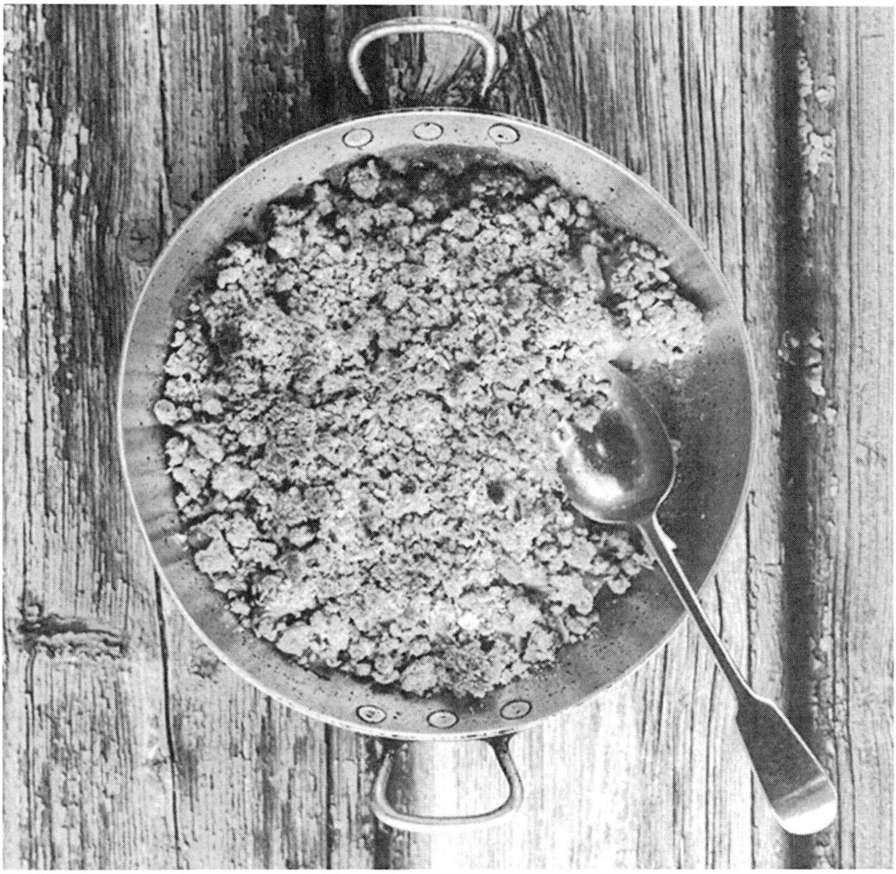

Cardamom & Cinnamon Poached Pears

Poached in warm spices and served with the reduced syrup, this is a great way to serve pears for a light dessert.

Serves 4

Ingredients:

    Water: 750ml/ 3 cups
    Light brown sugar: 200g/1 cup
    Cinnamon stick: 1
    Cardamom pods: 8
    Ripe pears: 4, peeled

Method:

1. Add the water, sugar, cinnamon and cardamom to a large saucepan over a low heat. Stir for a few minutes until the sugar dissolves.
2. Add the peeled pears to the saucepan, ensuring they're fully covered. Bring to the boil and then reduce the heat and simmer for about 30 minutes or until the pears are soft.
3. Remove the pears with a slotted spoon and set aside. Turn up the heat and bring the syrup to the boil. Continue to boil for 5–10 minutes until it's thickened.
4. Add the pears to bowls, drizzle the syrup over the top along with a dollop of yoghurt and some chopped almonds.

Stewed Rhubarb & Ginger

Tart rhubarb and spicy ginger are cooled with plain yoghurt. The chopped nuts finish this off well and offer a different, crunchy texture to an otherwise soft dish.

Serves 2–3

Ingredients:

Fresh rhubarb: 400g/14 oz, coarsely chopped
Fresh ginger: Thumb sized piece, peeled and grated
Caster/superfine sugar: 2 tablespoons (or to taste)
Dairy-free yoghurt: 200g/7 oz
Chopped nuts: A handful

Method:

1. Add the rhubarb, ginger, half the sugar and a couple of tablespoons of water to a saucepan. Cook over a medium heat stirring regularly. Once the fruit breaks down after about 10 minutes, continue to cook so that the mixture reduces and thickens. Add a little more sugar if required.
2. Serve in bowls, topped with the yoghurt and nuts.

Pineapple, Lime & Ginger Sorbet

Finish off your meal with the refreshing zing you get from these exotic fruits.

Serves 3–4

Ingredients:

> Fresh pineapple: 1, peeled and cut into chunks
> Fresh lime: 1, juice and zest
> Fresh ginger: Thumb sized piece, peeled and sliced
> Caster/superfine sugar: 50g/2 oz
> Water: 200ml/¾ cup

Method:

1. Blitz all of the ingredients together in a blender until very smooth, then pour into a container and freeze overnight.
2. Remove a few hours before required and allow to defrost slightly. Chop into pieces and blitz in a blender again until smooth. Add back into the container and freeze for an hour before serving.

Vegan Chocolate Brownies

Crispy edges and a gooey centre, brownies are something very special. Made here using only vegan ingredients, although that doesn't compromise the taste.

Makes 8

Ingredients:

    Gluten-free self-raising flour: 180g/6 oz
    Caster/superfine sugar: 180g/6 oz
    Cocoa: 60g/2 oz
    Coconut oil: 5 tablespoons
    Coconut soya milk: 200ml/¾ cup
    Vanilla paste: 1 teaspoon
    Pink Himalayan salt: ¼ teaspoon
    Chopped nuts: 30g/1 oz

Method:

1. Preheat the oven to 200°C/fan 180°C/400°F/gas mark 6.
2. Line a baking tray that is about 18 x 24cm in size with parchment paper.
3. Sift the flour, cocoa and sugar into a mixing bowl.
4. Melt the coconut oil in a saucepan over a low heat, then add to a measuring jug with the soya milk, vanilla paste and mix well.
5. Pour the wet ingredients into the dry ingredients and mix well.
6. Add the mix to the into the baking tray, scatter the nuts on top and then bake for 25 minutes until the brownie is just about firm. Remove from the oven, leave to cool. Cut into 8 pieces and serve.

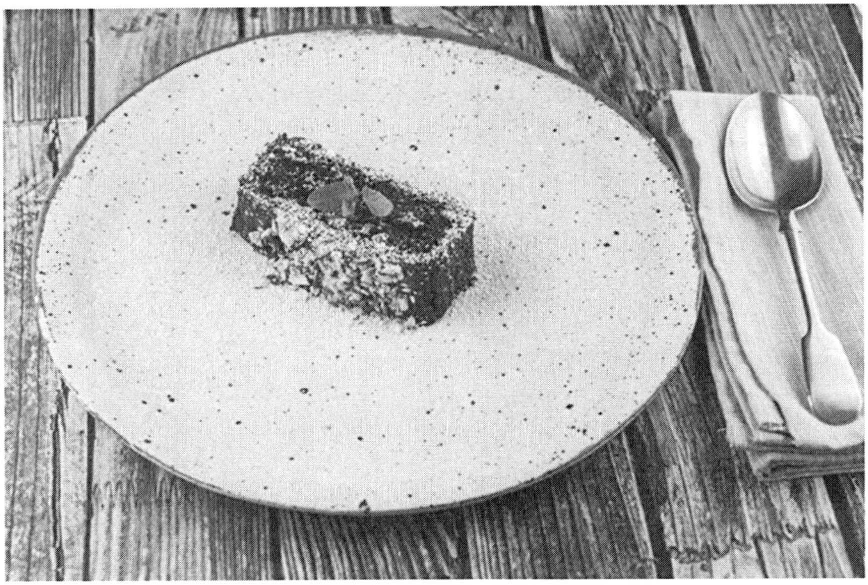

Basics

Gluten-Free Yorkshire Puddings

A homage to that old Yorkshire staple that used to be served as a first course to fill people up before the more expensive ingredient arrived – the meat. They go great with the lamb meatballs or classic roast chicken.

Makes 4 large or 6 small
Ingredients:

    Gluten-free plain flour: 55g/2 oz
    Corn flour: 55g/2 oz
    Pink Himalayan salt: ½ teaspoon
    Eggs: 2, beaten
    Dairy-free milk: 125ml/½ cup
    White pepper: ¼ teaspoon
    Olive oil: 2 tablespoons

Method:

1. Sift the flour, pepper and salt into a large mixing bowl and add the beaten egg and half the milk. Whisk until smooth, then add the rest of the milk and whisk again. Let it rest for 30 minutes.
2. Put a large muffin tray of 4 dividers with a touch of olive oil in each one into the oven and heat the oven to its highest temperature.
3. When the oven has reached its highest temperature, remove the tray and pour the batter into each slot, place back into the oven for 20 minutes until well risen and cooked. Do not open the oven during the cooking time or the Yorkshire puddings won't rise.

Gluten-Free Panko Breadcrumbs

If you've ever had something breaded in panko breadcrumbs, you'll understand the need to make a gluten-free variety. There are a few recipes in this book that call for a coating of breadcrumbs and having these to hand will produce much crispier results than using fresh breadcrumbs.

Any leftover gluten-free bread you have to hand.

Method:

1. Remove the crusts, then slice into 1-inch cubes.
2. Transfer to a food processor and blitz until you get a breadcrumb consistency. This will probably need doing in batches.
3. Preheat the oven to 170°C/fan 150°C/325°F/gas mark 3.
4. Spread the breadcrumbs evenly on a baking sheet and bake for 5 minutes to dry out.
5. Remove, shake the tray around and bake for another 5 minutes, then remove from the oven and allow to cool completely.
6. Store in an airtight container. They will keep for a few months.

Honey Roasted Vegetables

These vegetables are great served with the lamb meatballs, although they would also work well with pasta, couscous or baked fish. Feel free to experiment, both with the mix of vegetables and the dishes that you pair them with.

Enough for 4 as a side.

Ingredients:

    Butternut squash: ½, cut into 2cm squares
    Red onion: 2, cut into wedges
    Carrots: 2, halved lengthways and cut into 2 cm pieces
    Courgette/zucchini: 2, halved lengthways and cut into 2 cm pieces
    Olive oil: 2 tablespoons
    Clear honey: 2 tablespoons
    Fresh thyme: A few sprigs

Method:

1. Preheat the oven to 200°C/fan 180°C/400°F/gas mark 6.
2. Mix all of the above ingredients together in a baking tray big enough to hold them all, without overcrowding.
3. Bake in the oven for 30–35 minutes, until cooked through and caramelised in places.

Red Onion Gravy

This is a great accompaniment to the puy lentil or lamb shepherd's pie. The portion size could easily be doubled, with the leftover gravy frozen for another meal.

Serves 4

Ingredients:

    Red onions: 2, peeled and sliced
    Fresh rosemary: 2 sprigs, finely chopped
    Olive oil: 2 tablespoons
    Buckwheat or other gluten-free flour: 1 tablespoon
    Red wine: 125ml/1/2 cup
    Vegetable stock: 500ml/2 cups

Method:

1. Heat a large pan on the hob over a low to medium heat and add the oil, rosemary and onions. Mix well, season with salt & pepper and fry gently for 15 minutes.
2. When the 15 minutes are up, mix the flour into the onions, giving everything a good mix. Turn the heat up and add the wine. Cook for a couple of minutes then add the stock. Bring to the boil and cook for 10 minutes or so, until reduced to a thick consistency.
3. Serve with the dish of your choice.

Celeriac Mash

A great alternative to a white potato mash, with no compromise on flavour.

Serves 4

Ingredients:

    Celeriac: 1, peeled and cut into 2 cm dice
    Garlic: 1 clove, peeled
    Dairy-free milk: 300ml/ 1¼ cup
    Butter or dairy-free alternative: 1 tablespoon
    Flat leaf parsley: 2 tablespoons

Method:

1. Add the celeriac and garlic to a pan on the hob and add just enough milk to cover it. Bring to the boil and simmer for 20 minutes, or until the celeriac is tender.
2. Drain the celeriac and garlic, reserving the milk. Either mash by hand or add the celeriac to a food processor. Add a little of the milk and mash to the desired consistency, adjusting as you go. Stir through the parsley and season to taste.

Beetroot Pasta Sauce

This is a big recipe and one that I had to get right. It's a big recipe because a traditional tomato sauce can be used as a base for so many pasta and pizza dishes. The beetroot acts as a great replacement for the tomatoes, deep red in colour, sweet and earthy. You would really struggle to tell the difference between this and a traditional tomato sauce.

Makes 600ml/2½ cups

Ingredients:

- Olive oil: 2 tablespoons
- Carrot: 1 stick, diced
- Celery: 1 stick, diced
- Onion: 1, diced
- Garlic: 2 cloves, minced
- Dried oregano: 1 teaspoon
- Cooked beetroot: 250g/9 oz, chopped (or 250g/9 oz fresh beetroot, grated)
- Vegetable stock: 500ml/2 cups
- Apple cider vinegar: 1 tablespoon

Method:

1. Heat the oil in a large pan over a medium heat and add the diced carrot, celery, and onion. Fry for 10 minutes then add the garlic, oregano, beetroot and cook for a further 5 minutes.

2. Add the vegetable stock, give everything a good mix and simmer for 20 minutes.
3. After 20 minutes, add the vinegar, season with salt & pepper and then remove the pan from the heat and blend until smooth, adding more water if it's too thick. Check that you're happy with the seasoning, adding more salt & pepper if required.
4. This recipe can easily be doubled and then portioned into freezer bags so that you've always got the base sauce to hand.

Polenta Fries

With fries being so popular and with having to avoid white potatoes, we need a good alternative. I think I've done it with these, they're much better baked than fried as they become much crispier.

Serves 4

Ingredients:

    Polenta: 200g/7 oz
    Vegetable stock: 800ml/3¼ cups
    Olive oil: 2 tablespoons

Method:

1. Line a 20 x 30cm baking tray with cling wrap and set aside. Add the hot vegetable stock to a pan on the hob over a medium heat. Gradually whisk in the polenta, stirring continuously until well mixed. Cook for 2–3 minutes then season well. Tip into the tray, spread out and smooth the surface. Leave to cool, then cover and chill for at least 30 minutes, although it can be left overnight.
2. Preheat the oven to 220°C/fan 200°C/425°F/gas mark 7. Pour the oil into a baking tray and place back in the oven to heat up.
3. Turn the chilled polenta out onto a chopping board and cut into fries.
4. Add the fries to the baking tray and cook for 30 minutes, turning occasionally until crisp and golden.

Salad Dressings

The ratio that I usually apply to dressings is 3 parts oil to 1 part acid (vinegar or citrus). To complete the dressing, I'll add some flavourings and seasonings. In cases where citrus juices are to be avoided, use apple cider vinegar as a replacement.

Simple lemon dressing

Serves 4

Ingredients:

    Extra virgin olive oil: 6 tablespoons
    Lemon juice: 2 tablespoons

Method:

1. Mix all of the ingredients together until combined, season with salt & pepper.

Apple cider, honey and Dijon

Serves 4

Ingredients:

    Extra virgin olive oil: 6 tablespoons
    Apple cider vinegar: 2 tablespoons
    Water: 1 tablespoon
    Honey: 1 tablespoon

Dijon mustard: 1 teaspoon

Method:

1. Mix all of the ingredients together until combined, season with salt & pepper.

Tahini dressing

Serves 4

Ingredients:

Tahini: 3 tablespoons
Orange: ½, zest and juice
Garlic: ½ a clove, minced
Water: 4–5 tablespoons

Method:

1. Whisk all of the ingredients together until its combined and has the consistency of double cream, adding a little more water if required. Season with salt & pepper.

Creamy basil & chive dressing

Makes 125ml/½ cup

Ingredients:

Dairy-free yoghurt: 100g/3½ oz, sliced
Fresh chives: A small bunch, about 13g, sliced
Fresh basil: A small bunch, about 13g, sliced
Lemon juice: 1 tablespoon
Honey: 1 teaspoon

Method:

1. Add all of the dressing ingredients to a blender or food processor and blend until smooth. Season with salt & pepper.

Cumin & lime dressing

Makes 125ml/½ cup

Ingredients:

Ground cumin: 1 tablespoon
Ground coriander: 1 teaspoon
Extra virgin olive oil: 6 tablespoons
Apple cider vinegar: 1 tablespoon
Fresh lime: 1, zest and juice
Honey: 1 tablespoon
Dijon mustard: 1 tablespoon

Method:

1. Mix all of the ingredients together until combined, season with salt & pepper.

Kale Colcannon

A great alternative to the traditional Irish staple, using celeriac as a great substitute for white potato.

Serves 4 as a side

Ingredients:

Celeriac: 1, peeled and cut into chunks
Butter or dairy-free alternative: 25g/1 oz
Kale: 100g/3½ oz, chopped
Olive oil: 1 tablespoon

Method:

1. Boil the celeriac in salted boiling water until tender, about 20 minutes. Drain and mash until smooth.
2. Whilst that's under way, heat the oil and butter in a frying pan/skillet over a medium heat. Add the kale and fry for 5–8 minutes until soft. Mix in the mashed celeriac, season with salt & pepper and serve.

Almond Pesto

I love experimenting with different combinations when making pesto. This recipe isn't too different from the classic version. Great as a dip for some polenta fries or with spaghetti as a quick lunch. The recipe can be easily halved.

Makes 1 jar

Ingredients:

    Almonds: 125g/4 ½ oz
    Basil: 50g/2 oz
    Extra virgin olive oil: 125ml/1/2 cup
    Garlic: 1 clove, minced
    Lemon: Juice of ½
    Vegan parmesan: 50g/2 oz (optional)

Method:

1. Add all of the ingredients to a food processor and blitz until it's all mixed. When it's combined and smooth, season with salt & pepper. Keep in the fridge for up to a few days.

Mild Curry Powder

There isn't a curry powder on the market that doesn't contain chilli powder - Even the milder varieties usually contain some. So, as chilli powder is off the menu, I've created my own version. The good news is that it contains only ground spices, so there's no dry frying or grinding to do. Simply mix together and store in a jar.

Makes 1 jar
Ingredients:

    Ground coriander: 2 tablespoons
    Ground cumin: 2 tablespoons
    Ground turmeric: 1 tablespoon
    Ground ginger: 2 teaspoons
    English mustard powder: 1 teaspoon
    Ground black pepper: ½ teaspoon
    Ground cinnamon: 1 teaspoon
    Ground cardamom: ½ teaspoon

Metod:

1. Mix everything together and store in an airtight jar. It'll keep for up to 3 months.

Garam Masala

The spices used in garam masala vary greatly and don't always contain chilli powder so check the labels when you shop as it might be the case that you don't have to make your own. If, however, you can't find one that doesn't contain chilli, or you want to have a go at making it yourself, have a go at this recipe.

Makes 1 jar
Ingredients:

> Coriander seeds: 2 tablespoons
> Cumin seeds: 1 tablespoon
> Black peppercorns: 1 tablespoon
> Cardamom seeds: 1 tablespoon (seeds from about 20 pods)
> Fennel seeds: 1 teaspoon
> Cloves: ½ teaspoon
> Yellow mustard seeds: 1 teaspoon
> Cinnamon: ½ a stick (or 1 teaspoon of ground)

Method:

1. Toast the spices in a dry frying pan until aromatic and they've turned a little darker in colour.
2. Tip into a pestle and mortar and grind to a fine powder. Store in an airtight jar. It'll keep for up to 3 months.

Hummus

Most versions of hummus that exist on the market are really good, but it's so easy to make at home. I just had to include a quick recipe as the ingredients that are used here are commonly used in other recipes in the book, so why not have a go at making your own.

Serves 4

Ingredients:

    Chickpeas: 1 x 400g/15 oz can (drained but reserve the liquid)
    Tahini: 1 tablespoon
    Fresh garlic: 1 clove, minced
    Pink Himalayan salt: ½ teaspoon
    Extra virgin olive oil: 3 tablespoons
    Lemon: Juice of ½

Method:

1. Add the chickpeas, tahini, garlic, salt and lemon juice to a food processor.
2. Start the food processor and pour in the oil. Add in some of the reserved water from the chickpeas to get the desired consistency, it usually only takes a few tablespoons.
3. When fully combined and smooth, tip into a bowl, top with sesame seeds or za'atar and serve with some gluten-free pitta breads.

Pea & Broad Bean Hummus

A taste of spring, refreshing and vibrant when topped with some colourful radish. Also works well on bruschetta.

Serves 4

Ingredients:

    Frozen peas: 250g/ 9oz
    Frozen broad beans: 250g/9 oz
    Tahini: 1 tablespoon
    Lemon: Juice of 1
    Garlic: 1 clove, minced
    Extra virgin olive oil: 2 tablespoons

Method:

1. Boil the peas and beans in a pan of boiling water for 3 minutes, drain and add to a food processor.
2. Add the tahini, lemon juice, garlic, olive oil and a good pinch of salt to the food processor and blitz until smooth.
3. Serve with some gluten-free pittas and raw vegetables.

Black Olive Tapenade

Tapenade is a great little dip to have at the start of a meal with some gluten-free pitta and so easy to put together. All of the ingredients are simply added to a food processor and blitzed.

Serves 4

Ingredients:

Pitted black olives: 290g/10 oz jar (160g/6 oz drained)
Capers: 1 tablespoon
Apple cider vinegar: 1 teaspoon
Fresh parsley: 2 tablespoons
Extra virgin olive oil: 4 tablespoons

Method:

1. In a food processor blitz the olives, capers, vinegar and parsley until well combined. Gradually add the oil until smooth. Check the seasoning, adding any salt & pepper if required.

Green Salad

This is my go-to green salad. Packed full of leafy greens that are essential for healing psoriasis.

Serves 4

Ingredients:

- Celery: 4 sticks, sliced
- Cucumber: 1/2, halved lengthways and sliced
- Fennel bulb: 1, finely sliced
- Rocket/arugula: 100g/3½ oz
- Romaine lettuce: 1, sliced
- Spring onions/scallions: 4, sliced
- Grain mustard dressing
- Extra virgin olive oil: 3 tablespoons
- Apple cider vinegar: 1 tablespoon
- Wholegrain mustard: 1 teaspoon

Method:

1. Add all of the salad ingredients to mixing bowl and mix well.
2. Add the dressing ingredients to a cup, season with salt & pepper and then add to the salad.
3. Mix well and serve.

Griddled Courgette Salad

This is a great side salad to accompany a pasta dish or some barbequed meat or fish.

Serves 3–4 as a side

Ingredients:

- Olive oil: 2 tablespoons
- Gluten-free breadcrumbs: 100g/3 ½ oz
- Garlic: 2 cloves, minced
- Courgette/zucchini: 1, sliced
- Rocket/Arugula: 100g
- Fresh mint: 3 sprigs, leaves picked, finely chopped
- Extra virgin olive oil: 3 tablespoons
- Lemon: 1 tablespoon
- Vegan parmesan: A scattering

Method:

1. Heat a frying pan/skillet over a moderate heat and when it's hot, add a tablespoon of the olive oil, along with the garlic and breadcrumbs. Heat for a few minutes until the breadcrumbs turn golden, then add some salt & pepper. Continue to cook for a minute, being careful not to burn the breadcrumbs. Remove from the heat and set aside.
2. Mix the sliced courgette/zucchini with the remaining tablespoon of olive oil and season with salt & pepper. Place on the griddle pan and cook for 2–3 minutes on each side until charred. Set aside.

3. To finish off, add the courgette/zucchini to a bowl and mix with the breadcrumbs, rocket/arugula, mint, lemon juice, extra virgin olive oil, parmesan and serve.

Wholegrain Polenta

Polenta is a great alternative to white potatoes. I've previously used it as a replacement for fries, but wet polenta also works as a replacement for mashed potato.

Serves 4

Ingredients:

    Polenta: 200g/7 oz
    Vegetable stock: 800ml/3¼ cups
    Wholegrain mustard: 2 teaspoons

Method:

1. Add the hot vegetable stock to a pan. Gradually whisk in the polenta, stirring continuously until well mixed. Cook for a minute then stir in mustard, season with salt & pepper and serve.